MW01248268

The Divine Comedy

ACADEMIC INFERNO

My Academic Trip Through Adjunct Hell

The Divine Comedy

ACADEMIC
INFERNO

My Academic Trip Through Adjunct Hell

Virgil Henry

Accomplishing
Innovation Press

Academic Inferno
Copyright © 2024 Virgil Henry. All rights reserved.

4 Horsemen
Publications, Inc.   Accomplishing
Innovation Press

Published By: Accomplishing Innovation Press an imprint of 4 Horsemen Publications, Inc.

Accomplishing Innovation Press
℅ 4 Horsemen Publications, Inc.
PO Box 419
Sylva, NC 28779
4horsemenpublications.com
info@4horsemenpublications.com

Cover by Autumn Skye
Typesetting by Valerie Willis
Edited by Laura Mita

All rights to the work within are reserved to the author and publisher. No part of this publication may be reproduced, stored in a retrieval system, or transmitted in any form or by any means, electronic, mechanical, photocopying, recording, scanning, or otherwise, except as permitted under Section 107 or 108 of the 1976 International Copyright Act, without prior written permission except in brief quotations embodied in critical articles and reviews. Please contact either the Publisher or Author to gain permission.

All characters, organizations, and events portrayed in this book are a product of the author. All brands, quotes, and cited work respectfully belong to the original rights holders and bear no affiliation to the authors or publisher.

Library of Congress Control Number: 2023945653

Paperback ISBN-13: 979-8-8232-0316-6
Hardcover ISBN-13: 979-8-8232-0318-0
Audiobook ISBN-13: 979-8-8232-0315-9
Ebook ISBN-13: 979-8-8232-0317-3

DEDICATION

For the part-timers
You all know you do full-time work

TABLE OF CONTENTS

INTRODUCTION

LOST IN THE WOODS

HI. WELCOME TO THE ACADEMIC INFERNO. EVEN if your teacher never asked you to read Dante's *Inferno*, (or if you didn't read the summary online or Cliff's Notes depending on how old you are) you most likely have heard the phrase "rings of Hell" somewhere along the line. That is not to be confused with "Ring of Fire." That's a song that June Carter wrote for her husband. It's a banger, and you should totally go listen to that again sometime soon. Dante's *Inferno* is part of a longer piece that most people haven't read either called *The Divine Comedy*.

The story is about a guy called, oddly enough, Dante, who at the end of his life, is taken through Hell (*Inferno*), *Purgatory*, and eventually Heaven (*Paradise*). Sounds super funny, doesn't it? Comedy gold I tell you. Well, it was more of a social commentary and a satire. At the time of the writing, that was the definition of comedy. Today's comedy features a lot more fart jokes and dudes getting kicked in the junk than you will find in Dante's work.

Anyway, *Inferno* is the first part and the one more people read. Not because it's better but because it's a bit more symbolically rich. Sure, *Purgatory* can be an allegory too, but no one really uses that phrase much and people often confuse it with Limbo, which is that part of the afterlife that the Nazi Pope eliminated after he got a call on the God phone, like Popes do. Although, we will spend some time in Limbo in this book because it is in the OG material, so guess he couldn't change classic literature no matter how powerful his God phone. Either way, it really doesn't matter. *Purgatory* is exactly what you'd expect from a middle book in the trilogy. It moves the plot along, but it is rarely as good as the first. Plus, no high school teacher worth any salt would use *Paradise* as a way to teach symbolism. It's a bit too much on the nose. Still, we will eventually get to those in this series, but we will start where everyone starts, climbing down the rings of Hell.[1]

So, I decided to embrace my inner English teacher (I mean, I am an English teacher so I am just embracing my inner self), and I thought it would be loads of fun to write a collection of essays about academia, specifically higher education in the United States, using Dante's *Inferno* as a guide. Right now, we are in the introduction where we are lost in the woods and not sure what to do for a career. In a second, I'll get to that and how I decided to be a teacher. Then, we'll approach the gates of Hell and go down the rings one at a time. I'll tell lots of stories in this collection. All of them are true. Many will be about me, your guide, Virgil, named for the guide in Dante's book who was a great poet who wrote stuff you were assigned to read, but didn't. I am not a great poet nor has anything I've written been assigned in class so other than that, I am just like him. Some of the stories will be about my colleagues too. I'll drop in facts and figures to accentuate the points as we go, for the sake of credibility, but let's face it, the anecdote is what most people remember anyway.

I knew when I was in middle school that I would be a teacher. Two things happened. First, my grandfather, a farmer, said, "There are 2 things worth doing, farming and teaching." I looked at the farm he was about to lose because it was the 80s and having a small family farm wasn't profitable. I mean, he also was screwed over by a business partner some years before so that didn't help, but Reagan's policy on farmers was bad, and well, things were really fucking terrible. So, I looked around at the property where I broke bones and lost sleep and learned to drive a tractor, and I discovered I didn't want to eat meat, and I thought, "Well, this sucks."

---

1 Phillip Pullella *Reuters* Catholic Church buries limbo after centuries. April 20, 2007. www.reuters.com/article/us-pope-limbo/catholic-church-buries-limbo-after-centuries-idUSL2028721620070420

The second thing that happened was that I had a teacher who let me out of a class discussion on a book written by a stuffy British writer because I read it previously, but none of my classmates were reading it or cared to read it or wanted to understand it. So, she told me to go do something else while the other pre-teens fumbled around through the dense language and not-so-subtle symbolism about love and marriage.

I thought I would still honor the assignment and do something adjacent to the author's work, so I wrote my own, updated version of one of that person's different, but equally classic, works as a stage play for tweens. It was full of puns and was dumb, but for some reason, she loved it and let me cast it. So, I did just that. She watched it and laughed and somehow encouraged the principal to let us perform it. It was a big hit. We even took it on the road performing it around town. We were young vaudevillians, and we couldn't be stopped.

You might be asking, "Wait, why didn't you become a playwright then?" Good question. The playwriting didn't stay with me the most from that experience. What I learned most was that a teacher saw something in me and thought, *I know what to do to make that student learn even more.* She found a way to reach me when she didn't have to do anything more than let me sit in the back row, call on me when no one else would talk, and let me get an A on the test. Honestly, I'm not sure if I even took the test on that book. Let's just assume I did. I totally rocked it.

What I do remember was that experience, combined with the "pep talk" from my grandfather, mixed in with the love of books my mother instilled (she says "pushed") in me, and I realized that I could be an English teacher. I could inspire the next generation. Even if it sucked, it would have been better than farming. I was in middle school, so I couldn't see much further down the line so that meant I thought I would teach middle schoolers. I thought high schoolers were a possibility, but that seemed like a stretch. I mean, they seemed like giant assholes.

I carried this plan forward into high school, but then I thought I would teach English AND history because, you know, double the books, double the fun. Also, I had the world's greatest history teacher while one of my English teachers was a giant dick. So, that helped me go that way too. Of course, not all English teachers are self-righteous, megalomaniacs who ogled teenage girls; it was just I knew that one, and the thought of being like him was problematic. My world view was small.

Three years into high school, the plan was in place, and I was "lucky enough?" to have been elected as the student representative to the school board. Each year, we elected a member or two of the Junior Class to attend school board meetings. Our job was to give reports and to sit in and listen. We didn't have a vote, of course, that would have actually made sense. You know, asking the student body to have a vote and a voice as to what happened in their name. I'm not suggesting we should have had all the votes, but one, as a duly elected representative who could go back to the constituents, ask for input, have actual conversations, and inform the student body doing all the things that democracy is supposed to do would have been sweet.

So, while none of that actually happened, I did learn quite a bit about how high schools in America worked. All one must do is turn on cable news or open any random social media app to see how school board meetings look. Crazed people screaming and yelling at the school board over critical race theory (you say banana, I say, critical race theory is just the truth of history… what the actual fuck… shut your mouth you no-nothing idiot), or masks, and vaccinations (because working at the local food mart somehow makes you an expert on both topics), or books with two boys kissing (and the actual book *Two Boys Kissing* by David Levithan, which is very good and most assuredly banned in some school or 50).[2]

While those things were not happening while I was serving on the board, I most assuredly heard all kinds of crazy things uttered from "concerned citizens" and the school board members themselves. I watched my favorite teacher, the above-mentioned history teacher, have a book he selected be rejected, not because of cost, but because there was some stuff in there that might have mentioned that the United States lost in Vietnam, which was, spoiler alert, 100% true.

I watched for a year while people who had no background in education told people who dedicated years of their lives to

[2] *Banned Library.* Two Boys Kissing by David Levithan. June 3, 2017. www.bannedlibrary.com/podcast/2017/6/4/banned-99-two-boys-kissing-by-david-levithan

teaching young people that they couldn't have the resources they needed to enrich minds. However, the basketball team, coached by the above-mentioned, creepy-as-fuck English teacher, could have new uniforms every year because they were winners. Not like state champion winners, but winning record winners. Everyone loves a winner even if the winning percentage is like 50.1%. Keep in mind that the United States as a country has a winning percentage of like 99.5%, but that one book mentioned that America lost that one time, and that book was no good at all. Doesn't the team look great in those short shorts? It was the 80s.

I realized then and there that I was not going to want to deal with that stuff. By then, I knew people who were in college, and I discovered that 2 people could take the exact same class but could read different books and do different assignments because colleges had this thing called "academic freedom." Professors could assign books that said "fuck" in them or that told the truth. Classes didn't meet every day, and people only took 4 or 5 classes per semester. That meant that Professors were only teaching that many classes per term too! It meant that there weren't school boards full of people who didn't know the first thing about education.

Point of fact, there was a cobbler on the school board when I was in high school. This is a fact. A cobbler, for those who think it is a kind of pie (which it is), is a person who makes and repairs shoes. There was a guy on my school board who repaired shoes for a living. The 80s were wild. I mean the 1980s. I assume the 1880s were a mess too, and while they also had cobblers, I wasn't there because I'm not a time traveler.

So, my path was set in motion. I was going to go to college and become a college Professor. I was going to a college and Professors were literally in every building. I was in an area where there were HUGE state schools in every direction and community colleges in every county, not to mention, the small, liberal arts school that I attended and all its closest competitors. There were literally thousands of colleges and universities just in my home state. How many people were going to want the job? I knew lots of people, and I was the only person I knew who might even consider it. As far as I was concerned, I was going to have my feet up on some amazing desk in an office overlooking a lush, green quad before the new millennium. I was going to be in my late 20s on Y2K, and I was going to be OLD by then. When you are 16, 20 somethings have one foot in the grave. So it would make perfect sense that I would be all squared away as the new millennium rolled in.

HOW HARD COULD IT BE? RIGHT?

THE GATES OF HELL

COWARDS

Abandon all Hope ye who enter here.
Dante's Inferno Canto III Stanza 3

ROUGHLY 40% OF ALL WORKING FACULTY
MEMbers are adjuncts, and 75% of faculty have no path to tenure. That lovely little truth nugget only makes sense if you know what those words even mean. Let me explain. First, I'm not one of those douchey, ivory-tower types of "college folk" who feel the need to talk down to my reader, but instead, I'm a person who firmly believes that most of us don't know anything. For example, I don't know anything about how to fix a plane, fly a plane, load luggage into a plane, board people on a plane, open the door or close the door on a plane, or really, anything plane-related. Odds are, you don't either. That's why, when we fly, our flight crew goes through all the stuff you need to know each and every time. They know you don't know. They're not looking down on you, they just want you to feel comfortable. That's what I'm doing here. I'm the flight crew of this journey. Keep your seatbelts low and tight.[3]

So, faculty is what we call teachers in higher ed. Sure some K-12 folks do it too, but that's not as common. Why? It doesn't matter. It just is what it is. Not good enough? Fine. It used to mean something in which one was trained or qualified. It comes from

---

[3] Mia Brett. *Washington Monthly*. Adjunct Professors Need a Better Ground Game. September 17, 2021. washingtonmonthly.com/2021/09/17/adjunct-professors-need-a-better-ground-game/

there. Someone was trained to be a writer; she goes on and uses her faculties to explain her faculty and a whole new word for teacher is born. Of course, in academia, the word Professor is also bandied about. That word, of course, means one who professes knowledge, and so the faculty (not that horror movie with Jon Stewart. Why did anyone think he should be an actor?) is a group of Professors, professing their knowledge about stuff they were trained or qualified to do for a profession. Whew.

Professors are not all the same either. Nope. Some of them put on their pants one leg at a time while others pull both legs on at once. Really, the difference between them is not about pants but about rank although if different kinds of professors had to wear different pants, that would be amazing. Yes. Professors rank themselves. It's true. There's a whole rigamarole around it too.

The top of the pops is Professor. I know. Shocking. This is the only place in all of academia where saying it in fewer words is considered best. Sometimes, they will call themselves "Full Professors." As though, until they reached the pinnacle, they were only partial. I suppose that means we should offer the classes they taught before at a discounted rate or something. I think it means that students call all teachers Professors, and thus, they want to distinguish themselves from other members of the faculty. To have this title, one must typically have a terminal degree and have been doing the job for a while. It is typical but not universal. Some people get the title by working hard and/or licking boots, and/or doing just enough not to get fired for several decades. There are always exceptions.

"Terminal" here does not mean what you think it means either. It just means that in that field of study, there are no further degrees to be earned. Normally, folks with this degree are Doctors of something, but there are some degrees, such as Masters of Fine Art, that are also terminal. Some people think these degrees are equivalent, some don't. It's a whole thing and should, and could really, be the subject of another book (Virgil winks at his publisher).

Just below that is Associate Professor. The difference? Nothing as far as I can tell. As a person with that title, I see that I do the same amount of work, if not more, than the Full Professors. Really, it's just code in the industry for, "Been here a while. I don't totally

2

suck at my job, OR at least, I do a good job of keeping how much I suck hidden from sight." I put off getting the title because it seemed totally arbitrary, which it is, but I was told that if I ever needed to look for another job and I didn't have at least this title, it would signify I was difficult, or lazy, or both. I'm often difficult, but rarely lazy, so I got the promotion. It too was a whole thing. Folks with this title may or may not have a terminal degree. If they don't have a terminal degree or are not working toward one, the odds of becoming a Full Professor are low. It doesn't matter how good one is at the job at all. No terminal, no dice.

Next down the line is Assistant Professor. This is where most, but not all, full-time faculty members start. The title is a bit of a misnomer. Assistant Professors teach classes, write curriculum, serve on committees, and carry full teaching loads just like everyone else. They are not Assistants to the Professors as the name indicates. It is just a signifier to other academics that you are new on a job, don't have a terminal degree, or are difficult or lazy. Of course, some Assistant Professors do have terminal degrees but have not put in the time.

Below that are the rare cases of full-time employment as a faculty member where the person is not even given the Professor title. The job title for this level is Instructor. Students will call the person Professor either way. Instructors are often people who come into academics without any teaching experience but who do know the material, and they have at least a Master's degree. Think accountants and social workers who have done the job but never taught anyone. This is also a way for colleges and universities to pay these folks less for longer. They have to go through the promotion process to move up to Assistant Professors, and then up again and again. This starting title holds people back at least 5 years with lower pay while doing all the other stuff other faculty do. Totally makes sense, right?

Finally, way down at the bottom of the ladder are the adjunct faculty. The lack of capitalization here is intentional on my part. Adjunct faculty members are, on the whole, just as qualified as everyone already mentioned. The only difference is they are not full-time. They work on semester-by-semester contracts. They don't do committee work, write curriculum (not ordinarily, although they will occasionally. I know, I did, and I have asked some adjuncts to do so and I found a way to pay them), serve on committees, have to go to faculty meetings, or do most of the other administrative stuff that comes with full-time faculty jobs. They are generally paid between $1,000 and $5,000 per class with an average of $2,700. Personally, I never made more than $2,200 per class in all my time as an adjunct. Most of the time I made between $1,200-$2,000 dollars. They teach regular classes just like full-time folks and are considered high-quality experts in their field. They, for the most part (not always though), have the autonomy to teach the class as they see fit. Once the class starts, they are in charge of the course, and by and large, they are hard-working professionals. [4]

Many of them don't have other jobs. Sure, an adjunct in accounting may work all day as an accountant, and teaching is a side hustle. The same is true for people who work in marketing, human resources, or as vet techs. Lots of technical fields have a large adjunct population because it makes sense. However, there are no full-time historians just dying to work as an adjunct. Yes, it is the case, but those who work in the humanities and many who work in the social sciences are not full-time anything. They are full-time adjuncts. They cobble together classes from several places and eke out a living, working way more hours than every full-time faculty member does while earning no benefits.

Full-time faculty have lots of other responsibilities, but they usually teach 6-8 classes per YEAR to be considered full-time. This, like everything in the world is not universal. Some places do require slightly more courses per year, but in my experience, it has been 8 and I have never ever seen more than 10. That means on average, 3-4 courses per semester (much more on this in a later chapter). Summers are normally not required for full-time folks, and so the courses taught during summer are almost always adjuncts. Summer is a time when adjuncts can make a ton of money, but they do lots of work year-round. My personal record for one semester was 14 classes at 4 different colleges. I was physically in a classroom for 43 hours per week. That didn't count the

---

[4] Tony Guerra. *Chron*. The Average Adjunct Pay at Community Colleges. June 29, 2018. work.chron.com/average-adjunct-pay-community-colleges-18310.html

commuting, planning, student meetings, and grading. All of that said, I made less money than every full-time person I knew who worked during that same term. If I took out the food, gas, and all that other stuff I had to spend, I'm not sure I broke even.

It was so bad that one snowy night during that term I walked out of the back of a building at 10 p.m., having started my day at 8 a.m. in a different building at a different college 45 miles away, while teaching a noon and 2 p.m. class at a second-place that was geographically in the middle of those 2 campuses, and I had a terrible case of parking lot amnesia that we get at amusement parks or sporting events (or malls for those people who are old enough to know what malls are). I eventually found my car and made it home by 10:20 p.m., where I promptly collapsed so that I could start my next day, at 8 a.m. back in the same classroom I just left at 10 p.m.

My story is not unique. Adjuncts all around the US are doing this each and every term, and yet, they are considered disposable. If a full-time faculty member's class is cancelled, adjuncts are forced to give up a class to a full-timer. This once happened to me an hour (literally one hour) before the class began. It was a new course for me. I wrote a syllabus, read all the material, designed papers, and created a first-day activity. I put in easily 20 hours of work before the course, which only met for 40 hours over the course of the term, began. Of course, the school was super understanding about it and paid me for my 20 hours of pre-course work. They apologized profusely and gave me some sweet university swag, a cup of soup, helped me fill out the unemployment papers, and gave me a hug.

Just kidding, I was told, "Bruce needs to teach this class (this is his real name, but you won't know who it is, and I can't honestly remember his last name, so...) because his class didn't fill. We will totally have something for you next semester...or not. You never know, but if you file an unemployment claim against us for this, we will definitely not hire you back next semester Bye-ee." OK, they didn't say "Bye-ee" because no one said that back then. It was a simpler and yet more cruel time when people were huge dicks without so much as a sarcastic goodbye.

So, now that you have all that squared away, you need a clear understanding of the concept of tenure. Tenure is more common in K-12 schools in the US, but it still exists in some colleges and universities. Tenure means you are essentially bulletproof. You don't have to worry about your job forever and ever, amen. You can show up late, leave early, wear jammies, quit grading your tests, and do fuck all, and you will not be fired. Tenure is granted to someone who has been somewhere a long time, and has not, as far as anyone knows, done blow off the back of a prostitute while on college property. Depending on the place (especially larger 4-year universities), having a stellar publishing career helps.

That is not to say one owns a publishing company, but rather that one has written academic articles that have been picked up in some academic publication that no one reads, not even other academics unless they're picking up a copy because they too are published in that same issue. These articles are all interesting, earnest, and full of well-researched and well-reasoned ideas. You see why no one wants to read anything like that in this political climate.

Science folks and psychologists actually publish things other people want to read as they do studies that may advance the human condition in a real and measurable way. Those in the humanities may actually get a book published that no one will read. That is not to say the book is bad or boring, but it is most likely literary theory or something close to it. When was the last time anyone you know sat down to read a book, let alone one that was about literary criticism?

So, let's revisit that first sentence again, shall we? Roughly 40% of all working faculty members are adjuncts, and 75% of faculty have no path to tenure. If you are not tenured, you are on an "at-will" contract. Normally, the contract is renewed each year and could be cancelled at any given moment. I've seen this happen. People plan on teaching the whole year and find out in November that they will not be brought back in January. It is rarely for cause. It is just because, which is different.

I know, I know, most jobs are at will. Whatever it is you are doing has no guarantees. Professors should not be special. We are not special, but you know, we signed a contract and so we thought it mattered. Unless your parent owns the company or you own the company, or you have compromising photos of the boss doing something untoward on company property, your job isn't going to be guaranteed. So, you wonder, why would any faculty member have a guaranteed job? Well, that is a great question. I don't think anyone should have carte blanche in any job, and I'm not a fan of tenure. I don't think it's OK to be able to peak at 40 and just sit on your ass all day collecting a 6-figure salary while you recycle the same fucking boring bullshit lectures for 40 more years. The issue is that this tenure model does still exist and thus, in order to pay inflated salaries to the 25% who are blowhards who do nothing, (I know, I'm painting with a broad brush, plenty of folks with tenure don't blow hard, they just blow the perfect amount. I'm not writing about you) the other 75% of folks must be paid less to do more.

Of course, the person with tenure totally thinks s/he/y (this is the generic pronoun I will be using for this collection. I know it isn't a thing, but maybe I can make it a thing) deserves that job and all the sweet, sweet perks that go with it. S/he/y doesn't see the problem. S/he/y went through the shit and arrived at the primo spot, so why can't those other folks just shut up, quit whining, and do it too? If this process sounds a lot like the hazing that happens in Greek organizations to you, then you get it. It is just like that. Exactly like that. It is often humiliating, degrading, and full of mind-fuckery. However, the lure of being the person who one day can humiliate, degrade, and mind-fuck someone else is apparently super alluring… or we're all just masochists. Could go either way I suppose.

So, here we are at the gates of Hell. We know what awaits us now if we open them. We understand the journey, down the rings of *Inferno* where that tenured job awaits. Abandon all hope ye who enter here.

RING 1

Limbo and/or Ambition

Obscure, profound it was, and nebulous,
So that by fixing on its depths my sight,
Nothing whatever I discerned therein.

Dante's Inferno-Canto IV, Stanza 4

MOST FOLKS DO NOT BEGIN THEIR JOURNEY through the rings of Academic Hell with all the information you will garner in this small collection. Like Dante, most people who started the job could not discern anything. Earning the title of "adjunct professor" seemed like a big deal to me. The word "Professor" was there in the title. For most folks who want to join this team, they think once they've arrived, they have fucking arrived. End of story. Mic drop.

On my first day, of my first class, I was standing outside on a break with some other instructors. I smoked then. Lots of Professors still smoked in the 90s. I've long since quit, but I understand the inclination. I now settle for occasional day drinking. Back then though, smoking was a way to get away from everyone for 10 minutes. Other smokers are, largely, pleasant people. They'll share cigarettes. They have lots to say and they too, struggle to go upstairs. The wheezing is real.

Anyway, on that first day, a newly minted full-timer was there giving me her life story. I don't remember asking, but I was new, so I hadn't heard any of her stories. I was interested in hearing them all. I was green. I needed to absorb all the advice in addition to the first and secondhand smoke. Martha (yes, her real name, you don't know her) said, "It took me 7 years to get this job, but now that I'm here, it was all worth it."

The real-time me, who in hindsight was a stupid fucking arrogant asshole, thought Martha was obviously shit at her job. There was no way I was going to take that long to land a full-time job (I didn't land one for more than double that). The me from the future wants to build a time machine to go back and slap past me right in the face. I didn't even have a master's degree at that point. The fact that I was allowed to teach anyone with only a BA … less than a month out of college … was absurd. Someone should have been fired over that hire quite honestly. I was only a few years older than my students, and in most cases, I was younger than they were. Yet, my hubris made me think that Dr. Martha was somehow a fuck-up, and that was why it took her 7 whole years to land a full-time gig.

The first ring of Hell is Limbo. Yes, I know, Nazi Pope and all, but he wasn't around then and Dante wanted to remind folks that you might need to check your ambition at the door before you get too far in and you can't get out. He filled ring 1 with poets of great renown who thought highly of themselves and their work. They thought they were smarter than God, that's his whole thing. He ends up in paradise eventually and all. However, before he got there, he had to deal with the fact that he was also a "great poet." He was full of hubris. Hubris is almost always a problem. It will send you to Hell or get your leg torn off by a whale.

I didn't see my hubris, and of course, there was a time when I was so far down the path that I wanted to blame someone for not warning me. Of course, I had a warning. Right there on that first day. Martha, who had a PhD, who smoked like a chimney because it took her 7 years of working as an adjunct AFTER she earned her Doctorate to get a full-time job at a mid-sized community college where she taught humanities to a bunch of students who couldn't understand why anyone would study the humanities (or what that word even meant) was trying to tell me. I just had so much hubris stuck in my … let's say … every orifice that I couldn't hear her.

The thing is, even if I had heard her, it might not have mattered. For those who are in this realm, there is really nothing quite like teaching your first class. Even if one could understand all the hubris stuff, pulling off a successful course is a life-changing experience. I mean, I am most certainly a much better teacher now than I was then, but I did something great. I learned a password to a club that I had desperately wanted to know, and I was not let down when the secret door slid open and I stepped into that educational speakeasy. There was something incredibly appealing to being a "Professor" for the first time. I wouldn't say it made me drunk with power, but it might have made me slightly tipsy with joy. While it is true that many Professors do become drunk with power, that is normally not something that happens right away.

The reason many folks become teachers is because they genuinely love being in school and they genuinely love helping others. Sure, there is a small group of "If you can't do, teach" folks out there, and they are generally bitter assholes. You've met them. They talk a lot about their "other" jobs while in class. If you're in a business course and the teacher is telling you all about the time that s/he/y was the CEO of some now-defunct company, you're in for a bumpy class. However, if your Professor wants to actually "teach" you something about the subject matter and wants to share personal experiences to make your lives better, then you're in good shape.

Most likely, the person who shares those important life lessons was, like me, high on dopamine. Everyone has taught someone something. Every day, someone explains something to someone, and that person nods and gets it. For many people, that simple act is nothing more than a moment in the day. It is a thing you did because it was a thing that needed to be done. Most people forget that they even did it. It won't come up in the "How was your day" part of the evening program.

For those of us who wandered the woods and pushed the gates open, we were chasing a high. Helping other people feels amazing. Getting someone who says, "I hate this subject, school is stupid, you are stupid, and I hope you die" to eventually nod in understanding feels like winning the lottery. Teachers share that feeling with other public service folks, firefighters, librarians, nurses, and bus drivers, who do the work because it makes them feel something special and definitely not because they are making any money. That could be a whole other book too.

The reason ring 1 is Limbo is that the folks there still have a way out; the gates are just there after all. One could turn around and get out. The woods may lead that person to something else entirely. S/he/y could end up working in some other field or could get a teacher certification and teach in high school because, while there are all kinds of idiots crazy bombing the school board meetings, they will at least have a steady paycheck, and the insurance is usually great.

Remember though, ring 1 is also about ambition. Ambition is often given a bad rap. I get it. I grew up in an era when people saw Gordon Gekko say "Greed is good," and they thought it was a playbook instead of a warning. That happens a lot. The wrong people are idolized for the wrong reasons. That was why Stone made that second *Wall Street* that no one bothered to see. They didn't want to see the truth. The truth is hard and ambition is not always truthful.[5]

Ambition is optimistic. Ambition is what drives people to do crazy things like inventing self-driving cars, or giant penis rockets, but it also drives people to help. Anyone who drives 90 miles an hour in the direction of the accident has the ambition that s/he/y will save a life. The thing is, the EMT will not always save everyone, but that doesn't mean it isn't worth it for that person. That person will, after shaking off the bad beat, get up the next day and rush headlong into the fray once again because s/he/y is optimistic and feels that saving a life is totally going to happen that day.

Those who decide to turn their backs on the gates and venture further down the rings understand the inclination of the EMT. We don't see ourselves as saving lives in the exact same way as EMTs, but we do think that we can save lives in a different way. Higher education is a great equalizer. I have students who piss and moan that their degree is "just some piece of paper" and they need to "get a promotion or get the job they want." They complain that what I teach, those dreaded humanities courses, are a waste of time and on and on. Blah, blah, fucking blah.

Of course, they are contradicting themselves right there. That "piece of paper" is worth roughly a million dollars more than not having it. The "promotion" or the "dream job" is going to increase

---

[5] Oliver Stone. *Wall Street.* 1987 Twentieth Century Fox

their quality of life (well, most of the time). It will give people insurance (maybe, yes, that's a different book too, I mean, why does your job or the state in which you live have any fucking thing to do with insurance?) which means they can go to the doctor regularly and live a healthy life. They will have more money so they can live in a newer house and drive a newer car meaning that they're safer with walls built in this century and airbags in all directions.[6]

We see the *If You Give a Mouse a Cookie*-fication of education. Our ambition is not fueled at first by anything other than pure, unadulterated, un-cut optimism. For those who, like me, feel that learning how to think, how to write about what you think, and how to express those thoughts aloud, are valuable to the betterment of individual lives and to the world, we will never look back. On paper, we understand why people would see the rings of Hell laid out before them and decide to peace the fuck out, but emotionally, we just don't get it.

Thus, motivated fully focused ambition, off we go. We are the willfully ignorant fools out of Limbo and down the curved staircase into the next level, where getting out will be much, much harder.

---

[6] Kristen Broady and Brad Hershbein. *Brookings* UP FRONT
Major decisions: What graduates earn over their lifetimes
October 8, 2020 www.brookings.edu/blog/up-front/2020/10/08/
major-decisions-what-graduates-earn-over-their-lifetimes/

RING 2

LUST

Down to the second, that less space begirds,
And so much greater dole, that goads to wailing.
Dante's Inferno Canto V- Stanza 1

THE WALK FROM AMBITION TO LUST IS A SHORT
one and, often, the person doesn't even notice. It isn't because the
person really feels "lustful, lustful." No one wants to bang a syllabus,
and very few textbooks make anyone particularly randy. The way
that ambition turns to lust for those in ring 2 of this journey
through the hellscape of Academia begins with the first trip to
the campus where one sees the possibility of things to come.

To an academic, a corner office isn't the same as to a person who
is in business, finance, marketing, or something else that I don't
understand. To be fair, everything I know about most suit-and-tie-
type jobs comes from movies so that is to say, I don't really know
anything. To my understanding, the higher up one goes, the nicer
the office becomes, on a literal higher floor of the building, OR if
the building is small, the nicest office is the corner one because it
has more windows. In academia, the idea of having AN office is
appealing. I've seen plenty of folks who have "garden-level" (academic for basement) offices so they get an excellent view of feet,
dog balls, mud, snow, and lawnmowers at work. My first office was
inside a classroom. It was essentially a storage closet with a phone
line and internet connection. I would often have to whisper on
my office phone because someone was teaching accounting in the
classroom, and I didn't want to be a bother.

My next office was another closet in a different room in the same building. The next office was in the basement of a rented office building where 3 different departments had to share an open space (no, seriously). Desk, shelf, desk, shelf, just like all the way to the vanishing point. The big improvement from that was that the next year we were moved from that into open-topped, door-less cubicles. I could hear everyone else's everything all the time. Need to schedule maintenance on your car? Everyone heard about it. Need to get that yeast infection checked out? That's office information now. Did you order rotten calamari for lunch? Sweet. I was hoping I would get to smell that forever.

You're most likely saying, "Virgil, you said having an office was part of the lust. Those all sound like they suck super hard." You are right. They do all suck super hard. However, they are infinitely better than having no office at all. Wait, you may be saying, what about FERPA, that law where all student information is supposed to be private? How can full-time faculty have crappy, unlockable offices, and adjuncts have no offices at all? Clearly, that must be illegal. Wow, I can't believe you knew anything about FERPA. I mean, most students don't even know about it. That is a great question. Well... Hey, is that a Timber Wolf outside? I think it's an abandoned baby. We should go check on it. I'll bet it's hungry and wants to live inside.

At least I was willing to try to distract you with cute but dangerous wildlife. So, before I could teach my first class, I was told all about FERPA and how important it was, like super important. We could get shut down and lose our accreditation levels of importance. Don't post grades on a door. Don't hand back papers the old-school way where you have some student hand them back so everyone can see the grades. Don't put the grades on the front page of the paper; always have it on the last page so no one can accidentally see it if the student leaves the paper on the desk. Don't talk about grades in class. Do that in private. So, I was ushered into a soundproof booth that could only be accessed with my fingerprints, and it was awesome.

Seriously though, my first "adjunct bullpen" was one office that had 4 desks arranged in such a way that in order to use one, you had to stand on the seat to get in because the chair couldn't be

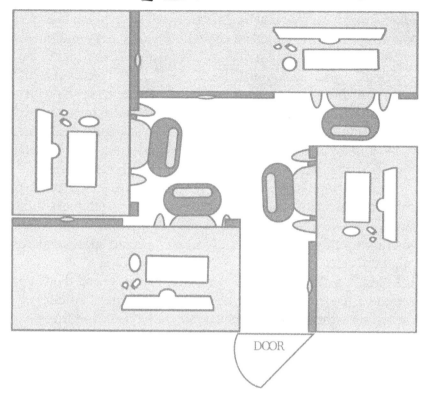

pulled all the way out because of how the desks were arranged and how small the room was. Below is a drawing of it.

Note where the chairs slid under the desks. The open spot on the bottom is the door. There was one HUGE overhead light that was roughly 7 billion lumens. The super-pasty members of the faculty could absolutely see the blood flow through their veins. There was a password-free computer on each desk. This room was shared by 30 adjuncts. Incredibly secure and obviously totally FERPA compliant.

Around the corner from this, there were the full-time offices. Our mailboxes were in there, so we all had to go in and covet their space. There was a lounge that was 3 times the size of our tiny closet and had free coffee and couches. We were "allowed" to spend time in there, but it was frowned upon if we spent too much time in there. "Get the coffee and get the fuck out." Besides, we didn't really like hanging around in there too much because one old-timer liked to tell dangling modifier jokes like they were dick jokes. I'm not making that up. I refuse to tell any of them here. Just knowing they exist should be enough for you to have nightmares.

Each full-timer had a desk, a table with 2 chairs for student meetings, a working door with a lock, AND several pieces of comfy furniture. One of my colleagues actually lived in his office for a while after his pregnant wife found out he had a pregnant girl-friend. This isn't gossip. This is a fact. Everyone knew he was living there, and no one really cared. He showered in the fitness center and ate in the lounge. He had a little fridge and microwave.

Some schools have slightly bigger rooms for adjuncts, but they call that the faculty lounge, and the full-timers often eat some funky crap they brought from home in there. They don't want to stink up their own area. Still, others have no space at all for adjuncts. They can set up shop in the library or at a table in the cafeteria. Most adjuncts teach at multiple places, and so, they carry around a ton of shit. The shit-carrying device most adjuncts go for are carts that are often shaped like milk crates, and they have an extendable handle like rolling luggage. I chose to use a huge backpack. I saw far too many spills happen in the parking lot or in the hallway when one of those tires gave out or when they had loaded the cart too heavily on one side, and it would topple going around a corner.

As sad as that is, or as funny depending on how big of a dick you are, you must keep in mind that adjuncts are supposed to guard all that private information with their lives, AND they can't talk about grades in public. Most colleges and universities do have "quiet" rooms in the libraries that they allow adjuncts to use for private meetings with students, but the ratio is usually 1 room for every 50 adjuncts, so look forward to doing student meetings at 6 a.m. or 9:30 p.m. They love that. It is super convenient. That means, most adjunct meetings with students are done at a table in the cafeteria during a lunch rush. The hope is that the din of people eating is loud enough to drown out anything too personal. I had a meeting once with a student in the middle of the afternoon. I'm sure no one heard anything important. Right?

Also, all of this means that every time an adjunct needs to get food, use the restroom, or do anything that involves getting up from the table, s/he/y has to make a choice. A. Pack up everything into the precarious rolling cart of doom and take it with, getting most assuredly urine and who knows what else on the wheels of the cart that will later be carried into the adjunct's home while risking losing the "good table" far enough away from both the door and the garbage, or B. Leave everything where it is essentially breaking several federal laws. The vast majority of folks opted for B because of that whole urine situation. Not me. I would leave my coat and hope that was good enough for me to claim my chair and stick everything in my bag. Backpacks are not just for kids anymore people.

There's a lot of humiliation that goes along with being an adjunct, but being lonely and in public, a person without a space, who is clearly treated like a second-class citizen while also being asked to impart wisdom and knowledge takes a lot of mental fortitude. What gets most adjuncts through it all is the fact that once class starts and the door closes, the room is ours for however long we are allowed. We have our backs to the board. Everyone's attention is on us. We are in charge. We are doing the thing we love. The thing we felt born to do. That room, once the door closes, transforms from being "a classroom" to "my classroom." Unless of course, there is a full-time faculty member hiding in the closet pretending it is an office.

RING 3

GLUTTONY

But when thou art again in the sweet world,
I pray thee to the mind of others bring me;
No more I tell thee and no more I answer.
Dante's Inferno- Canto VI-Stanza 30

THERE AREN'T A LOT OF PERKS OF BEING AN adjunct outside of how we feel as people for doing the work we love. I know, I know, that should be its own reward, but when you can only ever afford half a tank of gas, sometimes, you need a little something else. Of course, the something else we all want is to be paid better, or to have some sort of employment guarantee, or to have a tax break. While that seems like something unnecessary, it would be a huge game-changer for adjuncts. I have quite the story for you. However, we will go into that in the next chapter. Some may call that a tease, we in the tacher game call it a takeaway.

To offset the terrible pay, bad hours, and demoralizing treatment by the administration, colleges and universities love to give away swag. Faculty members, desperate for some kind of positive reinforcement, look to the swag bags as tacit approval of the hard work and sacrifice. This is bullshit of course, but when one is desperate, one will believe almost anything. Feeling like shit because the President keeps calling you Cary when your name is Carly? Wish that there was a spot in the faculty parking lot for you? Sorry, if you want one of those, you need to get here earlier. Guess you'll have to walk half a mile in the rainstorm to class. Good times.

Since I can't give you any of those other things, maybe I could let you pick from the magic cabinet of goodies. Will that work as a salve? Do you need a pen? Here you go. Hope you don't mind it has the name of the school on the side. What about a coffee mug? Yep. Have that too. Hat? Shirt? Gloves? We got you.

Here is a list of items I have been given over the years: pens, notebooks, folders, stationery, post-it notes with the university's logo on them, paper binders, mouse pads, flash drives, pennants, mugs, coasters (I am using one right now), shot glasses, wine glasses, beer glasses (clearly they think we need to drink heavily, which is accurate), tote bags, watches, those things you stick to the back of your cell phones to hold on better (what is wrong with our hands?), book bags, T-shirts, dress shirts, polo shirts (I passed on those because I hate them with a red hot passion of a thousand suns), sweat pants, sunglasses, gloves, baseball hats, winter hats, earmuffs, ear warmers (which are essentially thick headbands, the visor of winter apparel), snow scrapers, and I'm sure a billion other things I can't actually remember.

Sounds like a bag of cheap crap, doesn't it? Well, it is. However, when you're broke and starving and cold, you will take pretty much anything anyone gives you. I suspect that I could have clothed myself for years on end with just the junk I got from colleges. However, I never did get officially licensed undergarments. I feel like that is an untapped market. Although, I suspect if I were to look around online, I could find that people pay for officially licensed college bras, panties, boxers, and the like. OK. I just looked and wow. I never knew I needed a University of Tennessee thong, but now that I see it, I can't believe I didn't show my love before with a cloth string tightly pushed between my butt cheeks. What a fair-weathered fan I've been. Buy now.

Of course, the schools give this shit away as a form of advertising. This is nothing new. For a while there, The Gap and Polo, and every single store sold clothes that were both absurdly expensive AND acted as advertising and people forked over tons of cash for the privilege of wearing the company's name on their chests. How else could everyone know that you shopped at (fill in the blank name) unless your shirt had the name of the store emblazoned in 100-point font across the front? Of course, colleges want to do the same thing. It makes sense. People are, for the most part, super keen to take free shit. Every student who comes for a tour leaves with a bag of crap. Even cleaning your glasses with a micro-fiber rag (something I have and forgot to add to the list) must be a reminder of your campus visit. Now that you can see clearly, you can read the 10 thousand follow-up emails the admissions advisor is sending you.

Each year, the schools buy new crap to give to incoming or potential students and that means that faculty get the dregs and the adjunct faculty get the dregs of the dregs. Adjunct faculty are like the third-world nations who have shirts of the teams who lose in the finals. There are kids in some impoverished nations and lots of adjunct faculty who think that the Buffalo Bills won the Super Bowl 4 years in a row.

Yep, even as a full-time faculty member, I still take the gar-bage. It's just ingrained. I see a shirt, and I have to take it. Is that hat the world's ugliest shade of aquamarine? I'll take it. Don't need another (whatever it is)? Doesn't matter, I'll fucking take it. Is that shirt 2 sizes too small or 4 sizes too big? It's fine. I can give it as a gift or I plan on bulking up or slimming down (or both depending on how often I am paid and how hungry I am during a particular time of year, more on that in the next chapter as well). I currently have shirts that do not fit. I have them because maybe, just maybe, someone I hire will be that exact size, and I can send that person the swag, and I will be the best supervisor ever. If not, someone at Goodwill might be happy to find a shirt that has both the sticker indicating it is new and the logo of my university. Seems like some-thing someone would want.

While a fully stocked glassware cupboard is amazing, the thing that really gets the underpaid and underappreciated in academia going is free books. If you just peed a little out of excitement or if you had sexual arousal at the phrase, "free books," then you get it. If you are one of the zillion people who never read books, I would say for you to skip ahead to the next chapter, but then, you are probably not reading this either, so I didn't really need that warning. Away we go.

Publishers LOVE to give away free books to Professors. For some reason, they don't know or care about the hierarchy. They seem to think that every college or university allows Professors the ability to choose their own required reading lists (Where I work now, this is the case, but it is not the case in many places. In fact, adjuncts are now being dictated to more than ever. I know one person who was told she could design 10 percent of the course and the rest would be done exactly as it was designed by HAL, the malicious AI from *2001 A Space Odyssey)*. The book publishers are pretty thirsty for sales, so they give away poorly bound print copies and digital PDFs like the European invaders gave out booze and smallpox to Native Americans in the 1500s.

Most academics LOVE books. I have yet to meet a teacher who has said, "Book learning is for idiots." So, the opportunity to pick up a free book, even if you have no intention to read it OR if you have power or influence in the book-buying at your university, is compelling. I look at my shelf as I type this, and I see at least 4 books I have never opened, but I responded to the email from the sales rep with an enthusiastic "YES!" when s/he/y asked if I wanted an advanced reader copy.

If you combine the physically printed books with the e-books I get from publishers and from companies like NetGalley, who give me free books in exchange for reviews online, I would say in my 25-plus years of teaching, I've received over 1,000 books. Obviously, I don't have all of them any longer, but anyone who has creamed her/his/their jeans at the obligatory library scene (it's like porn for book lovers) in every single period drama will understand how hard it is to say no to books. Even if it means the free book ends up in the trade-in pile for the local book exchange or in the Goodwill pile (because throwing away books is a cardinal sin), we say yes.

I have books on subjects I am not remotely qualified to teach simply because someone wanted to give them to me. If there is a book I am barely interested in, I will ask for it because 95 percent of the time, the publisher says yes. They also know that 99 percent of the time, I won't use the book. Still, they give them; I take them.

In both of these exchanges, swag and books, the gluttony is on full display. The faculty member wants the stuff because, full-time or not, we don't think, or we know flat-out that we don't make enough money, so we want all the goodies to compensate. We think if we fill our shelves and cupboards and desks with free stuff, we have something that "normal" folks don't get (unless of course, they take a campus tour).

The colleges and universities think people will show up and pay an exorbitant amount of cash to be a student. The junk they give out is just advertising. It must work, or they would stop. The books, well, they are outrageously overpriced. Maybe if they quit giving so many fucking books away to adjuncts and full-timers, the cost for students would be lower. However, if they didn't give away a fuck-ton of books, the Professors wouldn't know about the new texts, and they wouldn't order them.[7]

As adjuncts, we justify it, and it just carries forward into who we become as full-timers. We are "owed" these perks, and by god, we're going to take each and every last paperclip and textbook. We don't care about the waste, or the cost to the students, or anything else. The companies and colleges don't care either. If 50 shirts they bought from a Cambodian sweatshop translates to one new student, it will all have been worth it. Gluttons each one of us.

---

7   Gaby Del Valle. *Vox*. March 6, 2019. The high cost of college textbooks, explained. www.vox.com/the-goods/2019/3/6/18252322/college-textbooks-cost-expensive-pearson-cengage-mcgraw-hill

RING 4

GREED

What is this Fortune which thou speakest of,
That has the world's goods so within its clutches
Dante's Inferno- Canto VII- Stanza 23

OF COURSE, GLUTTONY AND GREED ARE SIBLINGS

who like to hold you down and do that spit-dangling thing right over your face, so it makes sense that these 2 circles of Hell are so inextricably linked, and it's why I teased a bunch of stuff for this chapter in the previous one. All shall be revealed. I promise.

Before I get to all those promises (OK, I think there were only 2), I need to explain a bit about how one is paid in academics. I know I touched on this a bit earlier, but I didn't want to show off all my wicked math skills in one place. While it may seem like we are paid in magic beans that are planted in the soil of our dignity and lost dreams to be watered by the tears of those who came before us, we are actually paid in money (and the aforementioned swag). However, when and how we are paid is actually quite different.

Full-time faculty have more variety than adjuncts do. Most adjuncts are paid once a month OR sometimes not until the end of the term. That's a groin punch. However, some adjuncts are on the same rotation as the full-timers. Some places pay people twice a month. Once on the 15th and the last day. Some places pay once a month on the last day of each month. Some places pay every 2 weeks. Full-time faculty sometimes have an option of NOT being paid in the summer. That means that each check is bigger each pay period during the traditional academic calendar, which is typically mid-August through mid-May, but then they receive zero dollars in the summer unless they choose to teach (these are called "overload" because they are classes over the required load of their contract).

Why would anyone do this, you may ask, when the option of year-round, constantly steady money is available? Well, full-time faculty feel that since they are only contractually obligated to work those months, they are not required to work when off-contract. If you are getting your paycheck like clockwork and your boss calls you in July to ask you to do something, you may feel obligated to do the thing for free because, technically, you are getting paid for sitting around doing nothing.

The logic here is that if you're not getting a check, you don't feel any sense of moral duty to the organization even though you have most likely already signed your contract for next year, OR you are on a 3-year contract, OR you are tenured and have a lifetime contract, so technically you are still "working" for that college or university. It's not as though if you work at Target you don't work for Target on your day off. You are just not working that DAY. We all have been called in on a day off. To quote a different Dante, "I'm not even supposed to be here today!" (By the way, I have no doubt that Kevin Smith named his lead Dante with this poem in mind. There are 2 references to Clerks in the Greed section of the OG poem. Not the movie obviously; unless of course, Dante was a time traveler.)

Honestly, I am of 2 minds on this. I don't think it is totally out-rageous for your boss to want to talk to you about something that might take effect when you return when you are gone from campus for 12 weeks. There is this whole thing where faculty will use how busy things are in August as an excuse for not getting anything done. Of course, they will also say they are too busy in October and March because of midterms, in December and May because of the end of term, and in January because it is the beginning of the term. So, there is a sweet spot during one week in September, February, and April (not November though because of Thanksgiving break) where things can actually get done and new ideas can be put forth.

However, if the place of employment agreed to the contract that clearly states the faculty member is obligated to work from August

15th through May 15th, I'm not sure you can ask that person to do more without compensation. It's like when an athlete signs a long-term contract and then holds out the next year for more money or when someone signs a record deal, breaks it big, and wants out of the contract. I understand you are better now than you were then, but they signed you to a long-term contract because they thought you were going to be better. Your wanting to change terms mid-way is a dick move. I mean, we all know contracts really have no meaning anymore, except when we want them to. Remember when people could be taken at their word? What's that? That isn't a thing? Sorry. I'll smash my rose-colored glasses and move on.

The point here is, I can't decide where I land on the issue, so I decided to ramble a bit. Sorry. You should totally decide for yourself what you think is right. Maybe faculty contracts should be year-round. Even if one works year-round, there could easily be 6 weeks of built-in vacation a year due to semester breaks and holidays. Most full-timers get 3 weeks at Christmas, 1 week at spring break, and another week combined with Thanksgiving and Easter. Factor in the myriad of other holidays, and there are 5 plus weeks already. If one factors in a break after summer term and before fall term, plus July 4th and the time off surrounding that, we are right at or even over 6 weeks. Keep all of that in mind as you read on.

The average full-time faculty member makes pretty good money. It isn't great money, but remember, this person is being paid on average, $70K a year for a 9-month contract where s/he/y is asked to teach between 6-8 courses per year and serve on a few committees and maybe do some advising of students. Yes, this is the average. My base contract isn't anywhere near that, but if I had stayed at one place where I was in the teacher's union, I would be making well over that right now. I do pick up a lot of overload courses, and I teach year-round, so I do make nearly $70K, but it takes a lot of extra work to get there. I know lots of full-timers who make well into 6 figures and many, like me, will never make that much. Hence, the average. Here comes more of that sexy, sexy math.[8]

---

[8] *Glass Door.* How much does a Full Time Faculty make? September 15, 2022. www.glassdoor.com/Salaries/full-time-faculty-salary-SRCH_KO0,17.htm

An average course meets for 3 hours per week, and most faculty are required to do one office hour for each 3-hour course s/he/y teaches. Of course, some classes can meet longer if the school uses quarter hours or if there is a lab, but in the bell curve of teaching, 80% of classes fit in here. The shorthand is that teachers should put in one office hour for each class s/he/y teaches. Office hours must be posted and put on all syllabi. Faculty sit in their office waiting for students to swing by just in case someone needs help. Most of the time, the faculty member sits there and grades papers and works on other things to cut down on having to do it at home.

This is part of the contract. So, if one is only teaching 4, 3-hour classes, one is only required to physically be on campus 20 hours per week. Yes, there are faculty meetings and committee meetings and the like, but those typically take up another 5 hours per week on average. So, for $70K, one must physically be in one location 25 hours per week for 9 months per year minus the aforementioned built-in time off, so that means it is about 30 weeks per year…carry the 5, hold on…that means a faculty member makes roughly 94 dollars for each hour s/he/y is on campus if s/he/y teaches 4 classes per semester. Yes, faculty do have to do work at home sometimes, but it all depends on what and how the person teaches. If s/he/y gives out tests that can be graded by a machine and uses materials provided by the book publishers, well… you get the picture.

While I am not sure that 25 hours a week, 30 weeks a year, is super taxing, and I wouldn't know because I have been teaching year-round for over 25 years and I always, always teach more than the standard load, I do understand the reason for this schedule. The idea is that Professors need time to think big thoughts, do research, and write books and papers that they present at conferences all around the world. Some of these conferences are pretty interesting, and there is often a lot to learn from them. However, they are often scheduled in the middle of the term, so teachers need to get subs or cancel classes to go. It's fucking outrageous.

If they are not on the writing and speaking circuit, the idea is that Professors should be spending time investigating new texts and designing courses for the future, and thus, they need that extra time. We can all agree that time off increases creativity and productivity. On paper, it is beautiful, and it makes sense. In reality, many Professors use the same crappy lectures for 20 years in a row, only upgrading to new texts when they are forced to by the publisher and, even then, can't always be bothered to change the syllabus to reflect the new text. Most of them just use the time off to do whatever pleases them (mostly complaining about being underpaid) and still have the balls to take a sabbatical, which is a paid term off, to work on a personal project because their normal work schedule is just so overwhelming. You know, they couldn't possibly find time to write a book, or edit a book, or do a research trip, or speak at a conference with their 22 weeks a year of free time.

If that isn't the human embodiment of greed, I don't know what is. I can totally understand taking a paid term off to develop a new program for the university, or to re-write all the curriculum for one department, or to go on a recruiting tour around the country FOR the university. Sometimes you spend money to make money. If you pay someone to create an entirely new program in 15 weeks, you are saving literally years of time on the process if the person was designing the program while working a regular load. That means the program will come to fruition faster and money will be coming in. Win-win. However, I have yet to see the return on investment that comes from an obscure work of non-fiction that delves deeply into the economic impact of goat herding in 17th-century Ireland that no one will read, including the students at the university or the people of Ireland.

So, not only is the book a huge fucking waste of time and money because not only was the faculty member paid to not teach, an adjunct was also paid, not nearly as well obviously, to teach those courses in the place of the full-time Professor. So, the sabbatical costs the university even more money that they will not recoup. I get that not all education is about money, but it seems to me that the sabbatical is a huge money pit. Maybe the money could be used to pay adjuncts more, or maybe you could pay the campus security folks more or the lawn crew. I'm just saying, those people are actually showing up to work and contributing like 48 weeks a year.

Still, as fucked up as it is that some people are paid to not work but to write books and do things that have no use, what is more sickening is when people are paid not to work so that they can write books that they then force their own students to buy. I'm going to pause here in case you were speed reading or listening to this collection as an audiobook and zoned out.

Just to be clear. Some faculty are paid by the university to write books, and then they make said books required reading for their courses so the students are paying for books that contribute to royalties back to the faculty member. How fucked is that? Super-fucked. Fucked with a cape. One of my college Professors wrote books that other schools used. He wouldn't even let other people at his college use his books. His reason, and I will always remember this, was, "If students want to hear my thoughts on the subject, they can just take my class. I'm here. Those students, elsewhere, are not." Drop the fucking mic.

Sure, maybe some people think they don't make enough money. Yes, most people don't think they make enough money and faculty must have advanced degrees and they often spend a lot of money on those degrees. That is no joke. Advanced degrees cost more than undergraduate degrees, and as we discussed earlier, most full-time faculty have 2 if not 3 degrees. I have 3. My long-term goal is to be like Lilith on *Cheers/Frasier* and have all the letters possible after my name. Well, except for MD, no one thinks I should be a doctor. Never mind. Where was I? Right, money. Still, just because I don't make enough does not mean I can fleece the university out of money that could be used for something else. See, that's the problem with greed. Almost always, the person being greedy isn't taking from some giant corporation that is also greedy a' la those idiots in *Office Space*. Generally, the greedy person is taking from an organization that can't afford the losses, so the money has to be made up by charging the clients, in this case students, much more and paying workers, specifically adjunct faculty, much, much less. Greed is not good folks. It occasionally, not often enough, backfires on people, and of course, when it does, it is usually the person who can't suffer the blowback at all who receives it the hardest.[9]

As we learned already on this adventure, adjunct faculty members must do a LOT more teaching, they have no offices, and they are often driving from campus to campus trying to make ends meet. They are on campus way more than 25 hours per week, and

---

[9] Mike Judge. *Office Space*. 1999. Twentieth Century Fox

they make substantially less money while almost always working year-round. Those adjuncts who do this work as a side gig, don't really worry too much. They make $5-10K extra per year, and they are happy to have the money to use on vacation or to pay down loans. However, for most adjuncts who do this work for a living, they are often struggling. They too, though, have multiple degrees. They too are highly qualified. Without them, most smaller universities would go under, and yet, they are treated as totally dispensable. I know I repeated myself there, but it was important enough to bear repetition.

OK, now for the 2 things I promised to discuss in the previous chapter and how Greed plays a role in how adjuncts function. It seems, based on what I've written thus far, that Greed could not factor into any of this. Adjuncts can't be greedy. They are the victims. Au contraire mon frère. You see, while there are certain rules about how many classes an adjunct can teach at one place, there is no rule as to how many an adjunct can teach across the board. Hence the story I told in the first chapter about teaching 14 classes at one time. Keep in mind, 14 classes are equal to or just 2 classes fewer than what most full-time teachers teach in 2 years. 16 classes in two academic years is what is considered reasonable for the quality of the teaching and the physical and mental health of the Professor. I can assure you that adjuncts, for the most part, always put the quality of teaching over their physical and mental health and since they don't have insurance, they don't get help and that is why you may run into your Professor at the free dental clinic or at the bar trying to booze away the blues.

Still, there is one greedy thing that adjuncts do and the blowback is often unforeseen and crippling, and here, finally, I reveal the 2 promised things. Adjuncts often have 2 times of the year. The flush time and the starving time. The flush time is usually summer because full-timers don't teach very often, and there are rules in place to allow folks to pick up one extra class per institution during the summer without there being a hit against the Affordable Care Act. That means, for 3 months, an adjunct can teach a full-time load at one school and not be eligible for insurance. No idea how that made it into the act, but there it is. It is pretty standard for full-time adjuncts, that is people who only work as adjuncts and have no other jobs, to make $20-25K during the summer. Sounds awesome right? Well, hold on. I'll get back to it in a few paragraphs.

The starving time is from mid-December through the end of January. Mid-December comes into play because that is often the one time of year that adjuncts don't have to wait until the end of the month, or even the term, to be paid. Payroll folks want to get the fuck out of the office, so they pay the final payment of the year early. So, right at the time of year when most people are spending thousands of dollars on crap that no one asked for and no one uses, adjuncts go roughly 35-45 days without being paid. The first payment of the new year is rarely before the final pay period in January.

You may be asking, "Wait, if they make all that sweet cash in the summer, why not literally bank some to get through the starving time?" That is a great question. There are several reasons why this doesn't work. The first is that adjuncts are often living paycheck to paycheck and in debt. That extra money is already spent before it arrives. The second, and this is the most insidious thing, there are actually huge tax penalties for the flush time, and it is often during the next flush time that the adjunct pays the piper.

The deal is this. Each school takes out the taxes based on what the adjunct faculty member makes. So, if a person makes $10K at one school, the payroll person sees that the person is below the poverty line and will take out the lowest percentage of taxes during that time. No one can live on just $10K per year, so the adjunct works at 3 or 4 places cobbling together $30-40K per year. The teacher sees this possibility and pushes for more. S/he/y is only doing the job out of love and more work means more love and as a bonus more money. The dollar signs start flashing at the possibilities. Still, all this new "wealth" is pre-expenses. As we established, adjuncts have a lot of traveling costs, and those costs are not tax-deductible because adjuncts are both at will and not independent contractors. So, the adjunct just eats the traveling costs and the costs of the home office and all that stuff.

That is already crappy enough, but the biggest problem comes with the fact that the state and federal governments see that the adjunct has made 35 grand, which is technically a higher tax bracket, and so, all the taxes s/he/y has paid in are not anywhere near enough. Thus, when taxes come due in April, the adjunct has not paid in enough and owes more money. The adjunct now has yet another debt that must be paid because the government charges steep fines and interest for unpaid taxes.

The truth is, I was so far behind that, each year, I could not pay in enough, and then the fines rolled over and interest rolled over, which added new fines. I changed my withholding to the max amount, and it was still never enough. I couldn't afford to pay in more each month as I had to live and feed myself and my children. I did the only thing I could do. I made my tax payments each month and put my student loan payments on hold. That is much easier to do. Anyone can get a deferment at any time, but the interest piles up. I was adding to my tax debt and my student loan debt while trying to work as much as I could. I picked up even more classes at even more schools and that raised my rate of pay even higher, but that also pushed me into yet another tax bracket, and that meant that I owed even more because I was still only making between $10-15K at each place, and they were only withholding as much as they could be based on how much I made, which, wasn't enough.

The secret "upside" was that during my time as an adjunct, I was actually earning some retirement money because I was working for public schools. It took me 17 years of teaching 15-30 courses per year to finally become vested with the state. If I had been full-time, it would have taken 10 years teaching 8 courses per year. After I finally had one full-time job, at one school, with a steady income stream, I cashed out my retirement, paid taxes on that money, and paid off my tax bill that had been hounding me for years. I had a full-time job, no retirement money to show for it, and my student loans had grown even though I hadn't taken out another dime. Interest is a thing. As it should be. I don't think loans should be given out for free. If there had been some sort of tax loophole for adjuncts like there are for rich people who make all their money in the stock market, I would have paid my student loans off, and I would still have all that retirement money.

My story is not unique. This happens all the time. It is happening now. It's easy to blame the adjunct for being greedy because s/he/y made a lot of money in the summer or for taking on so many jobs just because s/he/y could, and there must be some personal responsibility there, but would those tax laws be in place if there were not so many loopholes? What would happen if there was just a flat tax? Imagine if everyone paid the same amount on everything s/he/y made? Like 15 cents on every dollar be it earned income or from investments seems reasonable. No one ever pays in at the end. No one ever gets a refund at the end of the year. Everyone just pays in a share of what s/he/y makes. If that person makes more, that person pays more. The end. We know that this will never happen because, as we know, lots of people at the top of the food chain think their kind of greed is good while fighting against tax breaks for those who are clearly feeding on the bottom.

RING 5

WRATH

Each one her breast was rending with her nails;
They beat them with their palms, and cried so loud
Dante's Inferno- Canto IX- Stanza 17

WELCOME TO THE MIDDLE OF THIS COLLECTION.

You have reached the point of no return. It will take you longer to go back than it will to go forward. Maybe, I don't know how long it will be until the end. Regardless, in the actual poem, Dante and Virgil spend Canto XIII crossing a river. It is scary. Having crossed it, they can never go back. Not that they really had that choice once they left the first ring, but there was always that feeling that they could turn back.

As for our metaphorical journey through the academic inferno, we have crossed our river and made it to the point of no return. We are in debt. There is the financial debt that was clearly explained in the previous entry, but there is an emotional debt as well. When one is beaten down over and over, there are several ways one can react. One can roll over and take it like an abused dog. This happens all the time. The mental well-being of most adjuncts is…let's be nice and say somewhere between not great and totally shitty. One can only hear so many times that one is not worth more than, say, a set of bonuses for the people already making the most money before one starts to believe it is true.

I've been there. I'm still there. Most everyone I know who works as a faculty member feels that way. Not everyone of course.

Many folks, who reside in the center of Hell, feel fine. They are the people who were bullied and think it is only fair to return the favor. They are, on the whole, terrible humans as made evident through the many stories shared here.

Not everyone rolls over. Sure, everyone keeps coming back for more, but many people get super pissed, and that anger manifests differently for everyone. Some people, as Dante explains, scratch themselves raw and beat their chests in impotent rage. While that is not a healthy way to express one's anger, at least there is expression. Maybe some people get a punching bag and beat it senseless. Others may go out and run. Others still end up back at the bar. There is a lot of drinking going on in this collection. Maybe I have a problem… Nah. I'm fine. I'm fine.

Often, the rage just bubbles up inside, and the person will allow the feelings to create a physical manifestation. I've gained weight and lost weight. I've drunk myself to sleep. I smoked packs and packs of cigarettes a day. None of these were super healthy. I did get a punching bag, and I have to say, that is pretty amazing. I always felt better afterward and passing out after a good workout is way healthier than after smoking 10 cigarettes while doing shots of Jäger. I know boxing is not for everyone. It's noisy and takes up a lot of space. If you do it wrong, you will break your hand. It's a whole thing. Still, 5 stars. Would highly recommend.[10]

We know that unresolved anger is stressful, and stress is terrible for the human body. Yes, the fight-or-flight response is excellent. We can lift a car and save a baby or run into a building to save a baby or other things that involve baby saving. However, when the baby is saved, we are supposed to relax. That's why after surviving a car crash, we sleep for a long, long time (I have survived many so I know first-hand what a life-threatening stress ball feels like). I know that being treated like shit isn't the same as surviving a head-on car crash, but the slights, insults, and outright macro-aggressions add up. Over time, it is a death by a thousand cuts.

---

[10] Dr. Louise B. Miller. *Psychology Today.* What causes anger and how it affects the body. July 16, 2020. www.psychologytoday.com/us/blog/the-mind-body-connection/202007/what-causes-anger-and-how-it-affects-the-body

Humans are really great at adapting to pain and adversity. It is what has made us evolution's darling. We figure out how to lose a limb, and we keep going. So, while each of those thousand cuts festers and grows infected, we learn to ignore it, and we move forward. The thing is, just like a person who has lost a limb, the way we move forward is different even if we want to pretend it isn't. Each of those mental slashes hurts, and thus, in order to alleviate some of the pain, people act out. Generally, these little anger storms can be written off as jokes, but the text is not jokey, and clearly, they are not intended to be funny. It might start with the adjunct reacting to an obvious slight, with some snark that s/he/y might have let go before.

In my younger and more vulnerable years (yes, I can use that line now as the copyright is up), when I was still just a part-time adjunct, that being one who still must do non-academic jobs to survive, I ran into the chair of my department while doing one of my other jobs. I had been working at that particular college for about 4 years. I had branched out to one other community college as well, yet there were no full-time offers. Realizing Martha might be right about things, I enrolled in a Master's program. I asked the Dean of Faculty for advice. He was the person who could hire me full-time, so I flat-out asked what I had to do for him to hire me. He told me that if I wanted to keep working for community colleges, teaching developmental education, which he thought I should, then a Master's in Education was the way to go. I took out more loans.[11]

Running into the department chair went something like this:

Anne: Hey Virgil. I didn't know you worked here.

Me: Yep, I'm not making enough teaching, but I sure would like to. (Desperation is super attractive after all).

Anne: I hear ya.

---

[11] F. Scott Fitzgerald. *The Great Gatsby*. 1925 Project Gutenberg edition. www.gutenberg.org/files/64317/64317-h/64317-h.htm

Awkward silence as I decide what that means. Is she giving me more classes? This was before the Affordable Care Act so universities could work adjuncts with full-time loads with no repercussions.

> Anne: Well, anyway, I need something small for my son's room. Can you help?

I was working at a carpet store. I sold her a good remnant at almost cost and sent her on her way. A few weeks later she called me into her office to say that she had to take one of my summer classes because a full-timer needed it. Not to meet load, just because he wanted to teach over the summer. It was the guy who was living in his office so making good choices was his strong suit. He decided at the last minute, and since there was nothing left on the schedule, and since she knew "I already had a job," she was taking it from me.

> Me: I already have a job?

> Anne: At the carpet store.

> Me: Did you get your English degree so you could sell carpet?

> Anne: Of course not. (She realized where this was going, but she couldn't pull out of the skid. She didn't say no, or ask why she said, of course not.)

> Me: Yeah, me neither. If I had wanted to sell carpet for a living, I would do that. I'm not though. I'm an English teacher who sells carpet on the side. I also write for a local magazine as a freelance writer. I know plenty of full-time writers who teach English on the side. Do you know anyone who sells carpet but teaches English on the side?

> Anne: No.

> Me: Guess I'm one of a kind then huh?

Let me sidebar here for a minute to say that there's nothing wrong with selling carpet. I was quite bad at it. I found it difficult talking to strangers all day about carpet. I didn't have a passion for carpet or for sales. Sales is an important job, and it is difficult. I'm glad other people do it. It was never my career. It was a job. I needed a job, and that was it. Also, I could see someone who sells carpet who teaches accounting, business, marketing, or I don't know, sales on the side. That would make a lot of sense.

That moment, when I snarked back at Anne, was the first time I'd ever done that. Up until then, I'd always eaten the crow and asked for seconds. It was clearly not the first cut, but it was the first one that elicited that kind of reaction from me. It would not be the last.

Anne and I also argued about books (I didn't think students should have to pay 90 dollars for books we were only using for one term), and my schedule, and a few other things. My student reviews were good though, and my success rate (that is the percentage of students who earn a C or higher) was the best of the adjuncts. Still, ever since I pushed back at her by making my snide remark, she didn't care for me, and the feeling was mutual. Things got ugly. We were not being rational. There was no reason for me to keep pushing her. There was no reason for her to be such a dick to me. Yet, that's what happened.

We worked out a truce of sorts. I requested to be sent out to the remote learning sites where I didn't have to see anyone I hated anymore. Most community colleges have main campuses and then satellite campuses in the surrounding communities that serve students who can't make it to the main campus due to transportation issues or work schedules. I spent a lot of time at those centers after my first foray there, and largely, the best educational experiences of my life happened there. They should be categorized as boondocks instead of remote; they are so hard to reach. Most full-timers hate going. It was perfect for me. My anger subsided, and I fell back in love with teaching.

The end. Everything is perfect now. Goodnight, everybody.

OK. Not really. The point is, that I love the job, but there are so many times where I take things so personally. It is hard not to. I take pride in my work. I assume if you are a non-academic reading this diatribe, you take pride in your work as well. You should. You don't want some asshole to come in and shit all over the work you're doing. There is a way to be critical and helpful, and then there's being a dick. We all know the difference. As teachers though, we walk that line every day. I've seen some seriously, outrageously bad papers in my day, and instead of writing "you suck!" on the back of the paper, I think of ways of showing my student what is wrong and why it is wrong, and (this is the most important part) I show him/her/them how to do better.

Sure, sometimes the student gets angry, but the student can see that I am coming at it from a place of support and not a place of mockery or superiority. Having been treated like shit, I know that I don't want to treat others that way. I wish I could say that there is a solution to all the anger that comes from being an academic besides either quitting or becoming a bully. I choose neither. I choose to write a whole book about the mean things that happened to me when I was an adjunct so that others can learn from my experiences and know how to practice self-care and when to walk away, and more importantly, how not to be a huge dick when s/he/y gets a full-time gig.

RING 6

HERESY

Fiercely adverse have they been
To me, and to my fathers, and my party;
Dante's Inferno-Canto X- Stanza 16

FOR DANTE, AND FOR MOST PEOPLE, HERESY

means blasphemy against the church. It doesn't just mean taking the Lord's name in vain. It means saying, writing, or even thinking things that are antithetical to the teachings of the church. For some folks, that means saying gay people should exist and have equal rights. For others, it means saying women should be allowed to wear pants and cut their hair. There are lots of ways to be a heretic. One of the most famous heretics of all time just started his own church so he could get a divorce. So… You know, sometimes it pays to be a heretic. There are like 80 some million members of the Church of England now. L. Ron Hubbard got the joke too, didn't he? I mean … yes, God is in that spaceship right behind that cloud.[12]

In academics, there are different kinds of heretics. Writing an entire book that shits all over the whole institution while claiming to love it seems pretty heretical to me. Yet, writing this book isn't the worst thing I've ever done. As I am sure you've noticed, Dante wasn't an idiot when he set up his rings of Hell in the order he did. Each thing leads to the next and to the next. The road to Hell

---

[12] History Dot Com Editors. *History Channel.* Church of England. September 19, 2022 www.history.com/topics/european-history/church-of-england

may be paved with good intentions, but the road through Hell is a bobsled track.

This would be a good time to bring up academic freedom again. This phrase means different things to different people just like actual freedom means different things to different people. Some people think freedom means shouting obscenities at the President while others think it means shouting obscenities at one's neighbor for shouting at the President. One group says it's free speech, the other group says it isn't, and before you know it, everyone is confused, acting like an asshole and punching Rand Paul. I mean, violence is wrong, but I understand the inclination.

Academic freedom is, depending on where you look, the idea that students and faculty and everyone on campus are allowed to practice open debates without fear or reprisal AND/OR that faculty members are allowed to do whatever the fuck they want, and the administration can't say shit about it. I know, I know, odd that one phrase could somehow mean both things and yet, it does. Just like lead is an element on the periodic table and an action one can take depending on the context in which it is used. Academic freedom is the same thing in that one way is written down, has properties, and makes sense from all angles, and the other can be as varied as there are people who claim to be leaders.

The reason we need to think about what academic freedom means here is that you would think that regardless of which version of it you think is real, there would be no way anyone could actually be labeled a heretic. If we are all supposed to have open debates about everything and apply pluralism to everything, then we should be totally free to say anything without reprisal as long as we can defend our points with cogent arguments and supporting materials. Additionally, if we were all supposed to do whatever the fuck we want in our classrooms, administration be damned, then again, heretical action is not possible. If there is no dogma, there can be no heretics, right?

Well, if you think all of that, then you have never worked in a bureaucracy. You see, organized anything is all about bureaucracy (I am super bad at spelling that word. I should have gone another way with this section, but it's all too late now). Religion, business, government, academia, and everything else that has an organizational structure is, unfortunately, full of arbitrary bullshit (see I found a way around spelling it there). There doesn't need to be of course. If someone asks, "Why are we doing this thing this particular way?" and the answer is "Because we do it this way" then you are in a bureaucracy. If the answer is "We do it this way because…" followed by several reasons that make sense and use the word efficiency or something approximating it, then you are not in a bureaucracy, and you are working for a well-organized company.

One thing that bureaucracies also have are lots of manuals that say nothing. They are vague, open to interpretation, and normally ignored until necessary (I'm looking at you United States of America. The Constitution is a bit of a hot mess and for the most part, people ignore it until it is convenient to pull out a pocket-sized copy. Just once, I want someone to unroll a scroll that is 20 feet long and shout "Size does matter!"). A well-organized company has a manual that is concise, clear, and used daily. There are steps to follow because they are effective. They do things a certain way to make sure there is no confusion. Everyone knows the guidelines, and if one doesn't follow them, there are clear action steps to be taken.

It may seem that the bureaucracy is better for one who doesn't like rules because no one is really paying attention, and if we don't break any small rules, we can break the big ones. Well, that was Julia's argument in *1984,* and she still ended up in room 101, didn't she? Everyone ends up there eventually. I mean, I am sure O'Brien thinks he won't, but he will because, in a bureaucracy, everyone is trying to play a game, or has a long con, or thinks s/he/y is smarter than everyone else. Bureaucracies are, you guessed it, Hell. That's why this book exists. If academia wasn't a fucking nightmare filled with nonsense directives, bullying, lies, wrath, anger, gluttony… Well, you got it. You're reading this book. Sorry.

The thing is, the more put together and well-run an organization is, the more likely it is that the people there can actually experience freedom. You see, if you follow the rules, you can do whatever you want. I know it seems counterintuitive, but it isn't. Let's look at the Covid pandemic, shall we? I know you don't want to, but it will prove a good point here. If, right from the jump, say in March or April of 2020, everyone stayed inside for 2 weeks, a mere 14 days, and let the essential workers have masks and gloves, and we left them alone to do their jobs, the pandemic would have ended because the virus would have fucking died. It wouldn't have had bodies in which it could live and that would be that. Maybe people would have needed to wear masks for a month or so afterward just to be sure, but masks fucking work. That's why people wear them in hospitals. Masks. Full masks over your mouth AND nose. Both parts. Wearing just over your mouth doesn't work even if you're a mouth breather. Fuck.

Instead, because most countries are not well organized, people didn't listen. They said "You can't mask freedom" or some other bullshit, and years later, as I write this, the pandemic rages on. There are fewer events to attend. Businesses have closed forever giving us fewer options for food. There is just less stuff now meaning we have less freedom to choose all because people didn't want to follow the simple fucking rules. Stay in. We know it sucks. Just do it if you can and if you can't. If you are essential, wear a mask. Please. Just fucking do that. For fuck's sake, no one asked you to carry a bag of rocks on your back for 2 weeks. AHHHH.

OK. Sorry. I know, that was no fun but the point is, when there is no order, there is chaos. When we think we're free, we are actually less free. In polite society, freedom comes from order. If we were all anarchists, there would be no roads, no schools, no libraries, no farms, no food, no nothing. Even wild "soulless" animals have order. They have society. They do things in packs. Yes, there are some solitary animals, but mainly, they've figured out how to make things work because it makes fucking sense. You've seen those nature documentaries where there's plenty of time to dick around and eat bugs and sleep in trees because, for part of the day, the animals followed the rules of the society in which they reside.

We need a society to live. We just do, and things are better for everyone when there is some fucking order to things. We don't all have to get along, and we don't have to love every decision. Still, if we have an honest debate, hear all sides, and then compromise on the rules, then we all have much more freedom than we would when someone who just doesn't like what you are doing for selfish, petty reasons makes up a new rule because the rules of bureaucracy say they can change the rules midstream.

The sad truth is the amazing, pluralistic version of academic freedom is a myth. Sure, it may exist inside the classrooms of many teachers. It exists in mine and in the classrooms of many a humanities Professor. In practice, outside of the room, it doesn't. The real, ugly truth is that faculty hide behind academic freedom. They say, "I can do whatever I want," but what they mean is, "I am doing whatever I want because my way is the right way, the only way, and if you disagree, I will fuck you up."

Jim Gaffigan makes a joke where he says that people see the way he looks and automatically assume he's racist. Unfortunately, I get it. I've been in that situation where someone who looks a lot like me started to make a snide remark about the local Pride festival. He thought because I was a straight person like him, I must also be a fucking bigot. I just held up my hand and walked away. Again, violence is never the answer, but we understand the inclination to punch someone in the mouth, don't we?

Academia has a similar problem. They assume that because you work in the bureaucratic hellscape, you must be part of the machine. They think you will automatically just get the "We do it this way because we do" mentality. They assume that you are willing to just go along with the bullshit until it is your turn at the top of the mountain/bottom circle of Hell for you to be able to design a course of your own and cover it with your own stink forever. It is an educational policy designed by dibs. "I called this course! I get to design it however I want, and you all must listen. I called it. I'm gonna lick it for good measure. Maybe I'll pee a little too… just in case." As opposed to, oh, I don't know, sound pedagogical and andragogical theory.

As far as I can tell from my 25-plus years of teaching in higher education, once a course is designed, that is what it is. If changes come to courses, it is almost always done for 1 of 2 reasons. The original course designer wants to do it and that person's stink is still fresh enough that it is allowed, or the accrediting body of the college or university says it must be so. It is rare that a course will change from soup to nuts (an old food expression that means from beginning to end because, at one point in the history of the

43

world, nuts were dessert. The phrase should be from soup to dessert, but again, we don't make changes because…) without there being some outside force involved.

Higher education is supposed to be all about thinking big thoughts and expanding one's mind, but often, those lofty ideals are taught by closed-minded assholes who are really creating a bunch of clones who will go on to regurgitate some worldview that makes the teacher happy. There are so many Professors who love nothing more than to hear their own ideas parroted back to them. The closer one comes to sounding exactly like the Professor, the more likely one is to earn a higher grade.

There are, of course, always idealists, like me, at every school. There are people who think, "I have a good idea, but that person's idea is also valid. Maybe I should listen and learn something. This is a place where people go to learn after all." A student who wants to look for that can do so. It takes work, and sometimes, students have to suck the exhaust of the terrible teaching bus and take a class from a mind-polluting turd. There is nothing that stops the student from putting in the effort to learn more on her/his/their own. I did it all the time. Even the crappy Professors have built their classes on a foundation of a good idea.

Professors like to be right. They like to be the smartest person in the room. It is an allure of the job. Professors are, on paper, the smartest person in the classroom. They are experts in the subject matter teaching non-experts the material. Sure, a student will know more than they do about lots of things, think back to the airline industry example from earlier, but the Professors know best about whatever this one thing is. They will die defending it, so when a colleague dares ask "What if we did it this way instead?" they suddenly go into fight or flight mode and do anything to protect their baby (nice call back there huh?) from harm. Well, suffice it to say, this idea of always being right spills over to the staff room from the classroom and we have the issue of "We do it this way because we do."

There's an understanding that one teacher will not call the other teacher's baby ugly, even if it is. The reason is s/he/y doesn't want to hear that her/his/their baby is equally ugly. This is how we end up with ugly curriculum, based on nothing but arrogance and pride instead of sound theory. The students are often left out of the equation because they are often seen as a means to an end instead of the end product, which is what they are.

I love going to graduation. I mean, I hate it too. It takes too long, and the guest speaker forgets it isn't about him/her/them, but I get a profound joy seeing students graduate. They are so proud of themselves, as they should be, and their families and friends are proud, as they should be. It is a great day. That's why I do what I do. Many of my colleagues, though, forget that's the point. Each individual faculty member is just one small piece in the puzzle of the student's life. Sure, some instructors become several pieces because s/he/y connects with a particular student and becomes a mentor/advisor/reference writer, but generally, faculty forget students and students forget faculty. That's just how it works. It isn't personal; it is reality.

Those of us who can accept this stark reality remain altruistic and do our best to create a caring, educational environment that moves students to that treasured day when they wear a gown and a square hat. We are happy to be part of each person's legacy by imparting some skill or lesson even if the person doesn't remember it. We know, and that is enough. Those who can't accept it decide to make the courses they teach a legacy. They don't actually care what the students learn. They love hearing their own ideas spit back at them. Most of these folks don't put a major focus on discussion because discussion is about sharing ideas. They lecture, they give tests, and they assign papers that can only be completed in one way. The "right way."

Being a person who would dare question this process is the most heretical thing one can do in higher ed. I mean, union schools look down on a person less for refusing to join the union than they do on a fellow full-timer or even worse, and adjuncts dare question the "why" of something or even more egregiously offer up a way to make a change. Change is not something academics like very much.

I have often been the person to ask why. To push back. To say no, and oftentimes, it gets me 1 of 2 things: I am either blackballed and sent to educational Siberia, where I teach at extension centers (which I love), or I have the crappiest schedule. I never really worried about being fired because, as I mentioned, I had results. It's hard to fire someone for being a pain in the ass when the person isn't really, technically doing anything wrong.[13]

More often than not, the second thing happens and honestly, I don't really mind it so much. The powers that be decide to turn me into a pariah. When one grows up as an introverted outsider, being shunned by the "cool kids" isn't a problem. Sure, it's easier to be at the big kids' table, but often, the kids' table is much more fun; it is where the good stuff happens. It's like that food fight scene in *Hook*. It takes imagination and a good heart to see what's really happening.

I am going to jump ahead in my career a bit to the first year of my first full-time gig because it works with my overall theme of this book. I have plenty of stories of being a heretic as an adjunct, and I would be remiss not to share one here just for funsies.

I was in a huge meeting full of English faculty both full and part-time as we were all invited to select the reading lists for the courses. This is one of those places that doesn't allow anyone to pick his/her/their own books, so s/he/y can be replaced at the last minute without a hiccup. I had to tell one of the head people in charge that her choice of *The Book Thief* for American Novels wouldn't work for that class.

Without letting me finish explaining myself, she went on a diatribe about how plenty of American books don't take place in America. On and on she went. It was a long while. She decided she knew my argument against the book and came ready for a fight. "The American experience is what matters, not the location of the book."

I agree with everything she said, but that wasn't the point. After she tuckered herself out, I said, "Right, on all of that, but Markus Zusak is Australian." Pin drop. "Why don't we use it in World Lit?" Believe it or not, I was actually invited back the next year, but I suspect it was because that was just "how we do things" for that meeting, and there was no real way to stamp my Evite with a VOID.

Anyway, I finally got my first full-time gig. I walked in the door, having not learned any lessons from asking why and calling bullshit for the previous 17 years, and I was immediately sent to

---

[13] Steven Spielberg. *Hook*. 1991. Amblin Entertainment.

the kids' table. I was being particularly pushy about the efficacy of teaching developmental reading in a shortened term. Keep in mind, if an adult is in a developmental reading course, it means that person is reading below the college level. Often, that person is way below. I've seen some students with a fourth-grade vocabulary doing his/her/their damnedest to learn. Trying to get someone from that level to college level in 15 weeks is incredibly difficult. It takes dedication from the teacher and the student. There is a lot of gnashing of teeth with a student like that, but it can be done. However, trying to do the same thing in 7 weeks is outrageous.

I had the following confrontation with the person who designed the course.

> Sally: Did you know that I am on your peer committee that decides if you get tenure?
>
> Me: No. I didn't even know that was a thing.
>
> Sally: It is.
>
> Me: And?
>
> Sally: You need the people on that committee to be on your side. I'm just saying.

She really wanted to save her ugly baby, and she wasn't above unveiled threats. It turned out that I was not the only person who was at the receiving end of her emotional shiv, so my pleas went unheard on that and on every single other thing that I brought up about teaching those reading courses. Each one had a ferocious mama or papa bear defending it, and I was simply a stupid camper lost in the woods.

I went through the rest of that year feeling pretty crappy about my prospects of long-term employment. I was pretty angsty, but the money was good, and I had good insurance. I just had to suck it up. It's what full-timers do. Shut up, play along, be rewarded. (Much more on this in the 9th ring, so I will leave it for now). I kept telling myself it would be better. It had to be better right?

Then I found out that the other full-timer who hired on with me left after that first year because that person didn't enjoy the bullying and the bullshit. Go figure. I was in a low place at the beginning of my second year and assumed I was the only one who gave a fuck. I mean, I assumed other members of my department would agree that Sally was wrong or that some of the other monsters in the department were terrible, but they didn't want anyone telling them that their babies were ugly, so they just went along with it all. I made the decision to use the Julia strategy myself. I was going to teach the courses my way and, in public, nod and smile. Obey the small rules and break the big ones. Sometimes, we risk Room 101 for the sake of humanity.

I settled into my first faculty meeting of the year with my secret plan in place and devised plans to take over eventually. I would go alone. I was going to be the John McClane of that university. I would take down all the Grubers; I just had to be patient. I was pleasantly surprised though at our first staff meeting when a new voice I'd never heard before said my favorite 3-letter word. She asked, "Why?" Hearing her say those words filled me with hope. There was someone who, like me, was willing to ask the question. She was a new adjunct, and she, like me, thought maybe students should come first. She thought maybe pushing speed reading and learning to skim and scan on struggling readers was a mistake. (It is a huge fucking mistake. Those techniques don't help students who struggle with reading. Those techniques only work for excellent readers who have very good recall, not for 40-year-olds who must sound out any word that has more than 3 syllables.)

She was promptly put in her place by Sally and her hangers-on, but I recognized that I might have an ally in the fight. It was very exciting. I thought, "Now I have a machine gun. Ho. Ho. Ho." OK. I didn't think that at all but wouldn't it be cool if I did? Instead, I found out her teaching schedule and tracked her down. I caught her between 2 classes, where she was eating her lunch in her room (no offices remember), and I told her that I agreed with her and shared some of the many harrowing tales from the previous year. She agreed to join the heretics anonymous club with me, and a friendship was created.

I didn't last much longer at that place. Like King Henry VIII, I just couldn't take it anymore. I needed a divorce, so I took a pay cut and found a new job. Right after I started the new job, I was asked to recommend someone to replace me as an adjunct. I mean, it would make sense to just hire both of us full-time, right? Right? So that's what happened. Just kidding.

I knew there was only one person to ask. My heretical pal. Over the years I have collected my own crew of amazing, albeit under-paid, adjuncts, and she is still with me. She does have a full-time non-teaching, academic job now, but she still loves to teach, and I am still lucky to have her around. She and I just recently gave up weeks of our summer to design a class we will only teach once. To this day, when I need an honest educational opinion, she is on the short, shortlist of people to call. She and I don't always agree, but because we believe in academic freedom, we have chats about it, and we work out good ideas that are best for our students. Unlike Henry VIII, my new group doesn't have 85 million followers, folks who are still considered heretics in the eyes of the Catholic Church, but those who are with me believe in what I am preaching whole-heartedly. Sometimes less is, well, less. Less is never more, but it is sometimes all we need.

RING 7

VIOLENCE

And when he us beheld, he bit himself,
Even as one whom anger racks within
Dante's Inferno-Canto XII-Stanza 5

I WANT TO BE CLEAR, AS I HAVE BEEN ALL along, violence is not the answer to anything. Again, while I understand the inclination, I urge you to get a punching bag, take a walk, scream into the void, do some yoga, cry uncontrollably until it becomes a really ugly, snot-faced cry. Any of that is better than committing any violence. OK? I mean it. We all have wanted to punch someone. Don't do it. You will regret it.

Interestingly enough, Dante spent a lot of time contemplating violence against others, as well as violence against oneself (he also spent way too much time and attention on sodomites which we will not do here because this isn't a book about how one spends one's time in the bedroom. Who gives a fuck what people do there? I don't). Of course, on the journey through the academic inferno, self-harm is a real thing. It is often mental, but not always.

I am not going to make light of self-harm.

It's bad.

If you ever think about harming yourself, please get help right away.

Please.

You are important even if you don't think so. *You are.* I promise.

I'm not going to skip this chapter completely even though I considered it. Shit is bad out there. Every day I read about some other horrific act of violence that happens. America is a violent place, and it's terrifying. I'm just going to make a crazy bold statement here, and if it turns you off, that's fine. Although, I suspect my rant about CRT in the intro would have precluded you from getting this far if you are a person who will be upset by what I am about to write. Guns fucking kill people. Guns are created for one purpose. They are designed to kill things and very often, guns kill people. They do. Yes, people pull the trigger, but they pull the trigger on guns. I know people will argue that violent acts happen without guns. Of course, they do. However, a knife attack, while also horrific, does not end with a double-digit body count. Fuck guns. OK. I think I'm done. It might come up again. I can't promise. Fucking guns. Fucking bullshit.

The thing is, violence isn't just physical, and violence doesn't always involve physical pain. It can, and it often does of course, but if someone blows up an empty building, that's a violent act. If someone hacks a company and holds it hostage for whatever the newest cryptocurrency, (Did I hear that there is something called Doggy Coin? That can't be right) that's a violent act. In academics, the most violent acts are those that leave no physical scars but have sudden collateral damage and have long-lasting effects.

A few years into my tenure as an adjunct, I got a call from the Dean who told me to go back to grad school. He said he needed me to fill in for a teacher who quit suddenly. She was offered a full-time job outside of academics, and she took it. She was still in the first ring of Hell, and she decided to get the fuck out. I think it was a job in advertising. Lots of English majors end up there. It doesn't matter. The point is, she was teaching American Lit I, which is American literature that was written in the space that is now the United States but before the founding of the country. The Dean felt pretty sure I was versed enough in the subject matter to jump in mid-stream. I was, and I did. Plus, I was doing him a favor, and when an adjunct can do a favor for a Dean, one does.

It was only an 8-week course, and I was coming in at week 3. If I didn't come in, the course would be cancelled because it was summer and none of the full-timers would take the class. Sit on that for a minute. This is the same place where a few years later, I would have a summer class taken from me arbitrarily, (also a financially violent act) but at that moment, none of the full-time folks could be bothered to give a fuck about the 15 students who paid to take a dense as fuck literature course in the summer. Summer students are, for the most part, the best. Unlike their high-school counterparts (I am not sure how accurate the Mark Harmon classic film *Summer School* is, but everything I know is based on that movie), college students who take summer school are trying to get ahead. They feel comfortable taking 15 weeks of subject matter in 8 weeks, and they just care a lot. I fucking love teaching in the summer; it is one of the many reasons that I teach year-round. More on that later when we come back to the self-violence stuff.

I look back on that course with fond memories because I think we all got through it with grace and had a positive learning experience. However, the fact remains that those students were shocked to walk in on week 3 and see me... and the Dean there. They felt betrayed. I spent the first hour just trying to convince them that nothing was going to change even though we all knew everything would. Sure, I didn't alter the reading list, but I didn't create any tests or quizzes and she didn't leave any behind even though that was part of her syllabus. I relied heavily on discussion, so the quiet students who were banking on earning points on a quiz suddenly had to push themselves out of their comfort zones and talk a lot more than they had originally planned to do.

Sure, that sounds like a minor thing, but if we follow the *If You Give a Mouse a Cookie*-fication principle again, we see that those students had lots of trust issues to get through for the remainder of their college terms. It is one thing when a tragedy happens. If something horrible had befallen the instructor, they could move on from that eventually. Instead, an instructor decided that those 15 people were not important. She didn't say goodbye. She didn't leave a note. Nothing. She just ghosted them (That term had not been invented yet, but bad breakups and no-shows at work were always a thing. I know it's hard to imagine a world without them, but it would actually be pretty great if we could get rid of them). That hurts.

It may seem trivial, but it isn't. Teaching isn't the same as working at Target. When someone quits Target, it affects those who work there more than the customers. Sure, there may be a customer or two who have a favorite cashier, but chiefly, the customers are unfazed. Teaching is, if done correctly, an interpersonal experience where the instructor and the students enter into a mutual agreement. The instructor will be firm but helpful, and the student will not be a huge dick when s/he/y gets negative feedback. OK. The nice way to say that is the student agrees to be receptive to that help and everyone grows and learns. This is the way of things from pre-k through PhD programs.

Teachers move on all the time. It is a job, and people are allowed to take better jobs, but generally, teachers move on after the semester or after the school year is over. Normally, they do not just quit showing up because the people who do the job, as we have established, actually care about their fellow humans. So, that is why when this happens, it feels emotionally violent to those upon whom the act is perpetrated. Please, I know, there are way worse things that other people have done in other professions, and there are way worse things teachers have done. This is not an apples-to-apples comparison because we never really ever compare apples to apples except when buying apples, and when we do that, there isn't a book of essays, or a reality show, or a 3-hour pre-game show designed to compare things that are sort of similar.

The point here is that the sense of abandonment is real. Students feel it. Every teacher that I know who isn't a huge asshole or who is further down the hellish journey than the first ring or two has agonized over looking for a new job because they feel this pain. Maybe it's that they've had a group of students who came up with them through a program and they want to see them finish up, or maybe it's that they think other teachers are sucky and will do a sucky job, or maybe they just feel a warped sense of loyalty to an institution that doesn't really give a fuck about them.

Still, on the whole, every single teacher will leave, and there will be a sense of rejection by those whom the teacher leaves behind. This is the case across all professions. We see it in sports all the time. When LeBron decided to "take his talents to South Beach" people lost their fucking minds.[14] People in Cleveland burned his jerseys and cursed his name. I have no doubt people wanted to do more than just throw rocks at his image and burn his jersey, things that actually happened because a grown man wanted to play a game in Florida instead of Ohio. Loyalty only goes one way. Instead of being a fan of a man who brought literally hundreds of millions of dollars to Cleveland during his first stint there (Yes, he went back, and all was forgiven until he left again. It's a whole thing, and I shall not be writing a book about it, but I am sure someone has and more people will.), people suddenly hated him to the point that they became vandals.

As far as I know, a teacher leaving one school for another, or even bailing mid-course has never elicited this exact kind of visceral reaction, but what is perceived as a violent act can come with a violent reaction. During my second year as an adjunct, I was doing an in-class exercise where students wrote for 5 minutes, passed the story along, wrote 5 minutes on that person's story, passed it along for 5 more, and then sent it back to the original writer who would finish it up. It was an exercise in quick thinking and writing through writer's block.

It's normally a pretty fun exercise, and students find it helpful. I like reading the end results to see how far afield the story goes from where it started and how the first writer pulls it back onto the road. It gives me insight into how creative/clever each student is, and it also shows me some writing tendencies. People like to use the same words and in academics that can *actually* (see what I did there) be problematic.

Anyway, when I was reading the stories over that night, I discovered that a few dude-bros thought it would be funny to write someone else from class into their exchanged papers where they committed violent acts upon said person. It was horrific. I took it to the Dean, and the students were removed from the course, although not expelled as I insisted, and they were told not to ever have contact with the person. The day after they were removed, I found a toilet paper roll in my mailbox that read, "You're a real piece of shit." It was stuffed with toilet paper. I wasn't sure, and

---

[14] *Associated Press.* Cavs fans upset with decision. July, 8, 2010 www.espn.com/nba/news/story?id=5365516

I still don't know if there was shit or a dead mouse or anything inside said stuffing. I showed it to the Dean who, as far as I could tell, did nothing. "Kids acting out" was his response. Nothing did ever happen beyond that, but it was not a fun remainder of that term. I never ran into those dude-bros again, so I assume they are doing time somewhere.

These are extreme examples and yet, at the moment, the actions that led to the reactions could not have been foreseen. If I hadn't done that writing assignment, those dude-bros wouldn't have done what they did, and I wouldn't have had them kicked out of my class, and they wouldn't have reacted with a not-so-veiled threat. If LeBron had stayed in Cleveland forever, lots of dude-bros wouldn't have ended up in jail for public intoxication and vandalism. We just never know what will set people off. It's pretty frightening.

Still, we must take action. Being inactive isn't OK. We have to do what we think is best for us even if that means we will cause some pain and suffering, even if it is only perceived pain and suffering, in others. However, as I have established, teachers play everything out and see the ripple effects of their actions every day; thus, they end up being inactive for longer than is necessary, and this is where the lower part of ring 7 comes into play.

Teacher guilt is a thing. It hits everyone differently. Do a quick search on your favorite search engine, and you will find rafts of articles about it. Some teachers feel as though they are not doing enough for their students, some think they are not doing enough for the college or university, others feel bad for taking a new job. It goes on and on. Guilt does a number on one's physical and mental well-being. To top it all off, most teachers are well aware that they are guilty and choose to do nothing but sit still and feel guilty.[15]

As an adjunct, I've shown up to work in a snowstorm that closed most roads except for the road to my college. Usually, on big snow days, the teacher and 2 students show up. Those students are there because they were already on campus due to a previous course, and they felt it was safer just to stay than to go home. I risked my life on more than one occasion getting to work only to

---

[15] Written by Kendra Cherry. Reviewed by Dr. David Susman. *Very Well Mind.* What is a guilt complex. November 8, 2022. www.verywellmind. com/guilt-complex-definition-symptoms-traits-causes-treatment-5115946

have the class be totally worthless. Most of the time, we just sit and chat about the readings and/or go over anything those brave few feel like discussing.

I've shown up with broken limbs, sprained joints, scorchingly high fevers, chills, runny noses, and my personal favorite, less than an hour after having a tooth removed. You see, I didn't have dental care and I had a cracked tooth, so the only thing I could afford was to have it yanked out. I actually felt much better than I had the previous 3 weeks when I showed up with a cracked tooth. Good times. Did it occur to me to stay home? Of course, it did, but I was an adjunct, and not showing up meant having my pay docked so that a sub could be paid with that money. Had I been full-time, I could have asked for, and received a sub. The sub would have been paid, and I would have still been paid.

Sick days are a real thing even though most Americans don't use them (or their vacation days if they are ever offered them) all up because they feel guilty, and the employers save a ton of money. This is a trend that goes beyond just adjunct and part-time workers, but it's even worse for them. They fear losing the money in real-time, but the job long term. Yes, it's more than just guilt, there's a sense of being seen as weak or as a slacker, but that just plays into the idea of harming one's self, doesn't it?[16]

There is a myth that a shit job is better than no job, but that is actually not true in all cases.[17] If one is too scared to take a sick day for fear of losing the crappy job, then why have it? The people there do not give a fuck. Workers are not seen as humans, but as a means to make money or to break even. Adjuncts are the perfect example of this. The average college course costs around $1,000.[18] This fluctuates of course, but it is the average. We established early on that the average adjunct makes $2,700 per class s/he/y teaches. So, that means with overhead and everything else, the college breaks even

---

[16] Brian Wheeler. *BBC*. Why Americans don't take sick days. September 14, 2016. www.bbc.com/news/world-us-canada-37353742

[17] Olga Khazan. *The Atlantic*. Is any job really better than no job? August 15, 2017. www.theatlantic.com/health/archive/2017/08/is-any-job-really-better-than-no-job/537969/

[18] Melanie Hanson. *Education Data Initiative*. March 31, 2022. educationdata.org/cost-of-a-college-class-or-credit-hour

roughly when 4 students take a course taught by an adjunct, and every student after that is $1,000 in profit. Many colleges say 7 is the magic number. They need 6 students to break even and 7 to turn a profit. So, let's go with that number. The average class size for an undergraduate course is 25 students, so that means the college or university makes 19,000, on average for every course taught by an adjunct.

Let's tangent here for a second, OK? That doesn't take into account the fact that sometimes, teachers, almost always adjuncts, will be asked to teach a directed study when the class does not meet the magic number. That means the faculty member is paid per student instead of a full rate. So, the students pay the full rate, but the faculty member usually makes 250 bucks per student even though the university makes the full amount. We all have done them because we care about the students and they need the course to graduate, but it really, really sucks. OK. Tangent over.

That means, the term that I taught 14 classes, the colleges I worked for collectively made $266,000 to my 37,800. I've established that I never made more than 2200 per class and during that time none of the courses I taught were above 2,000, but since we are dealing with averages, we will pretend. Those are the rules.

I ate a lot of fast food, suffered a lot of sleep loss, came to school sick on more than one occasion, lost personal time to read, write, reflect, or just enjoy life, all while racking up a huge tax debt and spending a lot of money on gas. None of those things were good for my physical or mental well-being, yet I chose to do it. No one made me. I loved the job. I still love the job. I wanted to do the work. As I said, while my own health suffered, my student's educational experiences did not. I gave it my all, even while taking 3 ibuprofen every 4 hours with a cracked tooth or 2 Dayquil every 4 hours when I had a cold.

There is a focus most teachers find when they walk into the room, and I always managed to find mine. I always put the student's first. I put the institution's long-term survival over my own. Look, I'm not naïve. I know that working in public services means less pay, more work, and an overall lack of respect from the community in general while also shouldering all the blame from the community in general. That's the job. The 7th ring is a violent place and yet, for those who've made it this far, we know the only way out is through and so down we go, beating ourselves on the back, trying not to crack up because we see that we are almost there. We are nearing the end where we get a full-time job and all of this will be better. The pain is worth it because I will be rewarded. Right? Right?

RING 8

FRAUD

But thou wast not so true a witness there

Dante's Inferno-Canto XXX- Stanza 38

YOU MAY HAVE NOTICED THAT THE QUOTE AT

the top of this section was 30 when the last one was from Canto 12 (We are using the Project Gutenberg edition just so you know). Well, the thing is, Dante really spent a lot of time with the whole sodomy thing as I mentioned, and that took up a few Cantos and then, when he got to ring 8, he created little pocket universes of Hell to show the different ways people commit fraud. It's long and he gets into lots of variants.

We're not going to do that here. Yes, it could be easy to tell a story or 20 about some faculty member who faked her/his/their credentials. People suck. I get it. We also could spend time digging into "for-profit" universities that entice students to take out tons of student debt for worthless degrees. There are a lot of those around, but the most famous is, unfortunately, the one that was eponymously named for the 45th President of the United States. You can look all that up if you want, but I don't recommend it. There is a whole system of checks and balances that are supposed to keep these things from happening; far too many people think regulation is a word that rhymes with smegulation and nothing else, so we have a lot of fraud there. I could actually write a whole book or 10 about this subject, and maybe I will one day, but that's not the thing I want to do here.

The biggest fraud I committed while teaching was that of omission. Sure, some will argue that being silent isn't the same as lying. That may be true, and I will leave it for philosophers and philanderers to debate. Odd how often philanderers get super philosophical about the meaning of things when they get caught getting blown by an intern in the Oval Office isn't it? If you want to watch your brain leak out of your eyes, watch the 42nd president say "It depends on what the meaning of the word 'is' is."[19] Seriously? That fucking guy. For fuck's sake man. I get so mad every time I see that.

Anyway, as adjuncts make their way down the rings of Hell and as full-timers consider which other moves to make, the biggest weapon they have is silence. In other professions, people openly state their grievances. Auto workers strike. Public school teachers in the K-12 system strike. Coal workers strike. As I wrote this, cereal makers went on strike. For those of you who also love Raisin Bran Crunch, I feel your pain. Some generic bullshit medley with raisins and dates and other random nuts is not the same. I'm still picking that shit out of my teeth, and I used a whole thing of floss. Professional atheltes hold out or demand a trade in the media. They may look like rich, spoiled dicks, but they don't have to hide it or, in the case of the US Women's National Soccer Team, they look like people trying to be paid what they are worth. Either way, they can make a stink because they have leverage.

In higher ed, talking openly about searching for another job is simply not done. There is no leverage, and while some people in education are spoiled dicks (as we have established and we shall visit this again in the coming chapters), that is not something that they can use in their favor the way athletes can and do. The way that adjuncts and full-timers go about this is different, and we will get into that here, but the reason they keep it quiet is the same.

Fear.

Yes, I know a one-sentence paragraph isn't a thing unless it's in quotation marks, but this is loosely based on a poem, I thought I could use some poetic license here. While there are currently jobs falling from the sky for those in the K-12 world, higher-ed jobs

---

[19] William Jefferson Clinton. *Bamageddrain on YouTube.* Bill Clinton It depends on what the meaning of the word is is. www.youtube.com/watch?v=j4XT-l-_3y0

are a bit harder to find. Well, let's say that full-time jobs are hard to come by. There are a ton of adjunct jobs out there, but many of them are location-bound, and no one should move across the country to take an adjunct teaching position. Thus, wherever the adjunct is, the jobs are finite. I cast my net around 100 miles from where I lived. I set my limit on a 2-hour drive. Yes, that is 2 hours each way, but I know plenty of folks who will drive even farther for the chance to get a foot in a door somewhere.

Just like any other job, one needs experience to be hired, and yet, until one teaches, one doesn't have any experience. Thus, first-time adjuncts often drive far, teach crappy hours, and do the courses full-timers simply don't want to do. Even though the open secret is that universities need adjuncts, they make them feel as though they are disposable. Seriously, if all the adjuncts stopped teaching tomorrow, shit would be bad in a hurry. In fact, there are some places where I've worked that rely so heavily on adjuncts that they outnumber full-time faculty 9-1. Even if the numbers are not that bad, we know from the beginning of this little ditty that 40 percent of all faculty are adjuncts. What would a nationwide walkout look like? Higher ed would grind to a halt. Sure. There are some schools at the low end that would be OK. Some full-timers could pick up an extra class here and there, but that wouldn't be sustainable because, as we learned, full-timers, for the most part, don't want to work as hard as they did when they were adjuncts. More to come.

So, why don't they all quit? It's the same reason they commit fraud every time they apply for a new full-time job or pick up another adjunct gig at the competing college across town. They think they will be replaced. There is a myth that there are clown cars of adjuncts parked in the back lot of every college or university just bursting with replacements. That's a big, fucking stinky, dirty lie. Sure, there are lots of people who "want to" adjunct or who think being called Professor sounds awesome, but when they find out they have to teach a course at 10 a.m. in one city and then 2 p.m. in another and 6 p.m. back where s/he/y started, that sounds shitty. It takes a person who is dedicated to the job, who has walked through the rings of Hell with us, to do that work. It is a special person. Teachers are special people both full-timers and adjuncts and yet, most administrations gaslight them into thinking that they are a dime a dozen. (A dime is worth 10 cents. It's a small silver-colored coin that people used to carry around in their pockets when they carried cash, which is like your debit card, but dirtier and with white guys on it). That is the fraud the university commits thus forcing the adjuncts into committing their own fraud. Lies snowball. It's just what they do.

An adjunct doesn't want to tell his/her/their boss that s/he/y is trying to get a full-time gig because s/he/y doesn't want to be left off the schedule. The adjunct wants to show loyalty to the person who does the scheduling and the university who gave them a chance and without whom a full-time teaching gig wouldn't even be in the cards. That old teacher's guilt rears its ugly head again. Remember, the school will pull the course at the zero hour for a full-timer to meet load or just because. Yet, they fooled the adjuncts into thinking loyalty is important. It is true that the longer an adjunct has been in a place, the more courses that person gets and the odds of being cut last minute plummet, but it still happens all the fucking time.

The other reason to remain silent is that often these full-time jobs happen at the last minute, and the adjunct may already be on the schedule to teach. They want to honor the students and the contract, but they also need the course just in case they don't get the job. It is like a slow, painful version of Chicken where the 2 cars are driving head-on at 3 miles per hour whilst being passed by jogging parents pushing strollers. The adjunct doesn't want to pull out of the job on a hunch because, let's be honest, no one expects to get that first full-time job. Most of us have been the first runner-up before. It is another part of the psychological horror that is working in higher ed. Always a fucking bridesmaid dressed in some ugly green thing that hangs guiltily in the closet in perpetuity.

When I was hired for my first full-time job, it was one week before classes were scheduled to begin. I was given the option to wait a term and start mid-year, but that would mean 4 more months of being uninsured and broke. Nope. I took the job. I was well aware that the courses I bailed on in the eleventh hour had students in them. The students in those courses bought books and read the syllabi and started preparing for my version of the course.

(Most likely not, that is another lie we tell ourselves in academics. We send out the syllabus and put book orders in early, but most students don't look.)[20]

So that is why adjuncts commit fraud. They don't want to lose the jobs they have, and they don't want to seem disloyal. Why then, do full-timers also commit fraud? Don't they have leverage? Can't they use the fact that another college might be interested in their services as a cudgel to get a raise or for better working conditions? Remember, they are the teachers at the university, not the highest-paid member of the university, the football coach. All too often, rumors are floated that X team is interested in Y coach, and then he (It is almost always a he who does this) goes to the administration and gets a contract extension and a raise even though that doesn't preclude him from taking another job later anyway and pretending he knows the fight song or that he has a southern accent even though he is from Massachusetts. (The first one was Bobby Petrino in Arkansas,[21] and the other was Brian Kelly at LSU, pretty fucking embarrassing).[22]

Faculty members know that there actually is a clown-car of folks who want their jobs. Most of them are the adjuncts they hired themselves. Many of them have as many years of teaching experience as they have. Some of them have degrees from more prestigious universities. The fear that if the administration got wind of the disloyalty and wandering eyes, they would easily cut bait and replace the full-timer with an adjunct on staff is real. Remember, only 25 percent of all full-time faculty have job security. They are at will. Here today, gone tomorrow. You think the grass is greener over there do ya? Well, why don't you go find out? Shove.

So, when a full-timer looks for a new job, s/he/y has to carefully select references from people who have already retired or whom they knew from a previous stint at another university. They

---

[20] Sara Smart. *CNN*. A professor hid a cash prize on campus. All students had to do was read the syllabus. December 18, 2021. www.cnn.com/2021/12/18/us/tennessee-professor-syllabus-money-trnd/index.html

[21] *Symms 2000 on YouTube.* Bobby Petrino's press conference Pig Sooi. www.youtube.com/watch?v=p7x3x6QHlrA

[22] *Top Fan on Youtube.* Did Brian Kelly fake a Southern accent at his LSU intro? www.youtube.com/watch?v=9f7XSv-CmKw

do interviews in secret during "personal days" or on holidays or while calling in sick. In my 25-plus years of teaching, I've never seen a new job be telegraphed to the administration ahead of time. There may be hints. I slowly took the few things I had in my cubicle home with me to make the getaway easier and quicker, but I've never seen the transition from one full-time job to another full-time job come as anything but a shock to those in the department. It always feels like a hostage removal from a crappy action movie every time. One moment the person was there, and the next, s/he/y was gone in a puff of smoke.

It's ugly, but it's the truth. The truth about fraud (That would be a great song name). I do my best with all of the adjuncts on my staff to let them know I don't expect anything from them except to finish out a term once it has started. I do think there is some loyalty owed to the students who have started a term with one particular Professor. Other than that, I tell them all that I don't have a full-time job for them, and I want them all to have one. I am a reference for each and every one of my adjuncts should they need it. I feel like I have broken the cycle of fear, and thus, we have broken through the dome of fraud that covers most departments.

I have a great relationship with my faculty, but I will admit, anytime I take a peek at the job listings at other colleges, (let's be honest, we all do it), I get a bit nervous. I mean, just because I've treated those like I would like to be treated, it does not mean that the administration where I work feels the same way, so after I look, I close my tabs and delete my browser history faster than a teenager who hears his/her/their bedroom door opening without a knock.

RING 9

TRAITORS

I care not to have thee speak,
Accursed traitor;
Dante's Inferno-Canto XXXII -Stanza 37

EACH PERSON THINKS S/HE/Y KNOWS WHO resides at the bottom of Hell. Each person thinks, "That crime is the worst crime of all." Many are surprised to learn that traitors are at the bottom. I'm sure that most people don't consider treachery the worst thing ever, but when you had someone cheat on you or break your heart, be it romantic or otherwise, you were pretty hurt and, at that moment, you damned that person to Hell. We've all changed allegiances. Things do change. Remember, Lincoln was a Republican as was Eisenhower. There is a zero percent chance either of them could win the nomination in today's Republican party. There are plenty of fair-weathered fans who root hard for a team when they win but don't show up when they lose. Some people were born and raised into a certain religion or not raised with one at all, and through education and personal experience, they change. I get it.

However, for most everyone else, there are 3 things about which one should be loyal until death and they are sports, politics, and religion. Sure, there are some hard-core Star Trek vs. Star Wars folks out there and DC vs. Marvel heads, but primarily, nerds just want to let other nerds geek out however s/he/y wishes. We have seen violence erupt over political leanings. We've seen violence break out at sports matches all around the world. Ask any Irish person about "the troubles" and you will hear all about how 2 groups of people who essentially have the same beliefs, hate each other. I mean, hate. However, if you asked people on either side of "the troubles" if they accepted Jesus as their personal savior, they would all say yes. If you want to read all about the absurdity of violence in religion, read Christopher Hitchens' book *God is Not Great*.

We will see more in the ultimate entry into this collection as to what happens to the worst of the worst religious traitors (it isn't pretty), and we can think about why Dante picked those guys, but for now, let's think about why it is that sports fans and die-hard political fans are huge dicks to people from the other team and, even more interesting, why they ostracize those who change sides. I promise it all ties back to higher ed. This isn't a different book suddenly.

Humans are social creatures. I mean, not all of us, but since we've been dealing with averages and majorities a lot in this book, we can't stop now. Even for those of us who are introverts, we still crave human interaction. Even if that means in small doses, we still need it. While it is true that opposites do sometimes attract and sometimes they even create long-lasting relationships, for the most part, people want to be around others who are like them. Sports and politics actually weigh more heavily than race or religion. One will see a United Nations of folks hugging and high-fiving at an athletic event or a political rally.

The Mets' jersey is so powerful that the devout Christian didn't even notice that guy had a Sikh turban on his head. Sure, my religion says you are going to Hell for not believing in my magic man in the sky, but it sure beats rooting for those fucking guys from the Bronx. Fucking Yankees. Sure, once the game is over, maybe that whole going to Hell thing comes back into play, but more likely than not, it won't come up.

There is a group of people called the Log Cabin Republicans.[23] If you don't know what that is, you most likely think it is a bunch of Republicans who love Lincoln so much they live in log cabins

---

[23] *The Log Cabin Republicans.* Home Page. 2023 https://logcabin.org/

and kill vampires just like he did. It's handy because of all the wood lying around. That would be a good guess, but you would be wrong. The Log Cabin Republicans are a group of LBGTQ Republicans. Let that wash over you.[24] This is a group of people who are in a party that led the charge for that ban of the *Two Boys Kissing* so much so that George W. Bush ran for re-election on the back of a proposed Constitutional amendment banning gay marriage. [25]

The need to belong to some groups totally outweighs the need to belong to other groups. The loyalty that these group members feel for each other is real. A Cubs fan would help another Cubs fan bury a body and frame a White Sox fan. A hardcore Democrat would look the other way when the leader of the party orders scores of drone attacks throughout his Presidency even though he ran as an anti-war candidate. One of those examples is 100 percent real and the other one is conjecture. Depending on your political proclivities, you will decide which is which. Either way, picking a team to support makes one feel like s/he/y is on the team. People say "We" (the caps are intentional to emphasize the royalty of the we) in reference to a win. Oh, I didn't realize you were on the ballot/or on the team. Congratulations?

Get back to the education stuff already. I don't care about this shit you are shouting right now. I get it. Hang on. I'm almost there. I need to get to the traitor stuff. Ask yourself this. What happens when a politician switches or leaves a party? What happens when the favorite son of say, Akron, OH decides to move to Miami? Fucking meltdown followed by violence and riots. Sometimes, it doesn't even take leaving the party but just speaking out against leadership. Looking at you Liz from Wyoming.[26] Thanks for your loyalty all these years, but it isn't good enough. You cheated. You left. You hurt us. Fuck you, you fucking traitor.

---

[24] *PBS News Hour.* President Bush endorses Amendment Banning Gay Marriage. February 24, 2004. www.pbs.org/newshour/politics/white_house-jan-june04-amendment_02-24

[25] Micah Zenko. *Council on Foreign Relations.* Obama's Final Drone Strike Data. January 20, 2017. www.cfr.org/blog/obamas-final-drone-strike-data

[26] Daniel Strauss. *The Guardian.* Liz Cheney removed from House leadership over Trump Criticism.

In the mob, or at least the movies about the mob, the worst thing anyone can be is a "rat." I suspect there are forty billion instances of someone uttering "I ain't no rat" or some variation of that across all of popular culture. The mob is portrayed as a family. In *The Untouchables*, DeNiro's version of Al Capone beats the shit out of a guy with a bat because he apparently let "the team" down.[27] Being a traitor will get you killed. It will get you booed. It will get you banned. It will, using the modern parlance, get you cancelled.

Being an adjunct is a lonely job. The adjunct travels from town to town, college to college with her/his/their little cart trying to make a difference. No office. No benefits. A person of no consequence to almost anyone at the university (except for you know, the most important people there, the students). While the time in the barrel is lonely, the experience is ubiquitous. Every adjunct everywhere has experienced something that I've mentioned in this book. Even if s/he/y climbed out while in ring 1 or just decided that abandoning all hope was not great for her/his/their mental health, there is something here that sounds familiar, and thus, the adjuncts are all part of the same team.

Like the sports fan or the political devotee, adjuncts bond because they have the same mindset. I've made it clear that no one does this job because of fame or fortune. Almost everyone who joins academia does so out of the need/want/desire to help others. They feel they have something positive to contribute. Sure, they may be pompous dicks who talk down to their students and their colleagues, but in their own way, they think they are helping.

When one is an adjunct, sure, the person is looking out for number one, but each day, the adjunct packs up the bag and the cart and gets into the car and heads out to make a difference. There is a sense of pride and satisfaction in helping someone else. When a teacher sees the student "get it" for the first time, everything changes. This experience, regardless of what one teaches, is the same. It is the glue that holds the community together. Republicans and Democrats can bond over knowledge. Math teachers and English teachers don't really speak the same language, but they are working hard for little money reaping only the reward of instilling knowledge that will bridge the language barrier. There

---

[27] Brian De Palma. *The Untouchables*. 1987. Paramount Pictures

69

is a common language. There is a sense of family and of being on the same side. Adjuncts empathize with each other and support each other.

When I was an adjunct, I tried to create an "off-the-books" sub-pool. I'll sub for you today, you pay it forward and sub for someone, and eventually, when I need it, someone will sub for me. The idea is that we had to band together because none of us could afford the pay reduction for that one class, and it must be really serious or we wouldn't need a sub anyway because, as we know, like the US Postal Service, adjuncts are hard to stop. It didn't always work because adjuncts are fucking busy and odds are, they don't have a few hours to spare to teach your class because they are on the road to teach classes somewhere else.

Still, for all the kumbaya moments that exist, the plan has always been to quit the team. As soon as one steps foot through those gates and agrees to begin this journey, the treachery has begun. Adjuncts who are friends and who share ideas, who volunteer to sub a class, and who have a friendly debate about pedagogy over lunch, will eventually, if things go well, join the dark side without a second glance back toward the light.

Those who are without sin, you may cast the first stone at the giant mural of LeBron James. Those who've never changed their minds may cast aspersions at Liz Cheney.

Every full-time adjunct has wanted from the beginning of time, and shall want for all eternity, to take his/her/their talents to South Beach.

Being on team adjunct is essentially like being on the Junior Varsity or even worse, the middle school team. You think you have the skills, but you are stuck down there. We all say we would rather play in the minors than sit the bench in the majors, but if that were true, House members wouldn't run for Senate, and Senators and Governors wouldn't run for President. They would be happy with where they are, and they wouldn't be looking to jump ship for seemingly better waters and a bigger booty (using the pirate meaning here).

I know I did it. The whole time I was on team adjunct, I was thinking about how to move on. I coveted the corner office, or any office, really. I wanted full-time health care, stability, a lighter workload, a pay raise, a reduction of stress, and even the prestige that comes with the title of Assistant, or Associate, or Full Professor. The whole time I was sitting with the other adjuncts, being part of that team, I was "talking to" the full-timers. I secretly applied for those jobs. I stayed loyal to team adjunct until the big breakup. Sure, I didn't cheat, but I was a traitor.[28]

---

[28] Oliva Rodrigo. *Sour.* Traitor. 2021. Geffen Records

CENTER OF HELL

I did not die, and I alive remained not

Dante's Inferno-Canto XXXIV-Stanza 9

FOR DANTE, GOD WAS GREAT, AND JESUS WAS
his personal savior. The whole point of *The Divine Comedy* was
to find salvation. So, it only makes sense that in the center of
Hell, where the shining morning star himself resides, we find him
chomping on Judas. Literally. His head is in Satan's mouth. Yep.
That Judas. The one who betrayed Jesus. Judas is one of those names
like Adolf or Barney (although for vastly different reasons) that has
been tainted by history. People will even say, "S/he/y is being such
a Judas" when referring to someone whom they feel has slighted
them in some way. I think that is a bit of hyperbole unless the
person calling the other person a Judas ends up crucified. Maybe
you should take that shit down a notch.

Brutus and Cassius are also there getting slobbered on by
Lucifer. It is nasty. Why are they there too? Well, like Judas, they
were the best friends/right-hand men to the big guy, and in the end,
they turned. On paper, they all turned for self-centered, self-ag-
grandizing reasons. Power, money, and a seemingly better life.
Sound familiar?

It could be argued that Judas did exactly what Jesus asked
him to do and he was actually the best friend ever. I often see
Horatio this way. He stood by and let Hamlet destroy himself even
though he could have stopped it because it was what Hamlet said
he needed to do. That may be an unpopular opinion, I understand.
Still. Worth considering is all I'm saying.

Anyway, the real point here is that those who end up here, in
the mouth of Satan, put themselves there by turning on the person,
or people, who helped them get to the top (or bottom) depending

on how you see it. It is literally a deal with the devil. Power and glory in life for a face full of Lucifer's acid reflux for all eternity. Is it worth it?

Well then, that is the real question, isn't it? When a full-timer takes a tenured position, what does s/he/y gain, and maybe more importantly, what does s/he/y give up? I suppose each person has to answer this question him/her/their self. Tenure almost always comes with a guaranteed raise each year. Imagine if you only had to do the bare minimum each year, and you still got a raise. Seriously, no matter what you do, you get a raise. I mean, don't kick a puppy (at least not on campus), and you will keep your job and get a healthy raise for working 25 hours per week for 30 weeks of the year. You will get this in perpetuity as well. You will never be asked to retire. That would be hard to turn down. You might even turn your back on everything and everyone you ever knew to hang on to a job like that. I mean, who cares if you call me a traitor, I'm on a 12-week paid vacation each summer.

I was there. I was looking at tenure right in the face. I had one more year of the bullies and the bullshit. I mean, Sally was awful, but was she that bad? I was good at the job after all. My students learned from me. I was following the small rules so that I could break the big ones. I could eventually design my own courses over which I could rule for decades to come. I just had to do a few things I didn't like. I had to eat some shit. Everyone eats a little shit now and again. It is the way of things, right? Twenty-two weeks of vacation time a year sounds fucking amazing, doesn't it? I mean, that is 22 weeks away from Sally. Can't I just do this for that? I'm already here. I already turned my back on the adjuncts I knew to take this job. I fucked everyone over who was counting on me that term so that I could start the job I had worked 17 years to get. I mean, what is one more year of indignity right? The money is so fucking good.

Tenure was the dream. Only 25 percent of all faculty members in the whole country achieve it. Job security forever. If the department I worked for closed, they would have to find me another department. If that department closed, they would have to pay to train me to work in a different department. Top-of-the-line insurance. Free travel to conferences. Did I mention the days off? It was like I was being rewarded for the trip through Hell. I could be the one to take classes from adjuncts and treat them like shit if I so wished. I could schedule myself into a 3-day workweek. I could make sure I only taught unpopular classes so I never had more than 10 students per course. 8 a.m. reading courses do not fill up. Whatever I wanted was just there, shining and seemingly perfect. Something I wanted the way Gollum wanted his precious (There is no doubt Tolkien read a lot of Dante).

However, the problem is, that once you have the tenure, you are still at the bottom of the tenure pile. While you can't be fired, the bullies and the monsters can't be fired either. They actually only get worse. They beat you down because they were beaten down. They say terrible things to each other without a second thought. I can't tell you how many meetings I sat in watching 2, fully tenured, Full Professors talking about each other through the department chair as though it was a bad sitcom. It was insane, yet the allure was still there.

Jobs like these come with what many call "golden handcuffs." I never heard this term until I was on the tenure track. One of my colleagues, who had moved to my state to take this job a few years before, was offered a job back in her home state at a pretty big research university. The university is solid. It has an excellent academic reputation. Most of the student-athletes not only graduate, but they graduate early. Seemed like a no-brainer to me. She, too, was feeling the weight of the job on her, and she was tired of the bullies and the assholes. She noticed that she was starting to talk like them and think like them. The indoctrination was almost complete. When I asked her why she didn't just jump at the job, she said, "The golden handcuffs are on me. I won't leave. You won't leave. No one leaves."

Sounds like the plot of a horror film, doesn't it? Well, maybe it is. Think about it. The public-facing term for the time before tenure is "tenure track." That means there is a specific route one must follow. Races take place on tracks. The tracks may be circular, or oval, or even look like a Rorschach test, but in the end, it goes around and around in the way it was designed to go in one direction only. Once one gets off the track and one has seemingly won the race, one is locked down with golden handcuffs. The only way to survive is to become one of the baddies. Be a zombie or vampire or ghost and live forever in an endless loop where new ideas are not welcomed and nothing ever changes. The pay though is exceptional. Even if you seem to be alive, you are not. *Groundhog Day* isn't a comedy; it is horrific. No one gets out of here alive. Abandon all hope. Even when you get your dream job, it will suck the life out of you, and there is nothing you can do. Don't have dreams. Thanks for reading. Shit sucks.

Wait! Isn't there always a final girl at the end of a horror movie? Bill Murray got out of his time loop, didn't he? (I am pretty sure his name is Phil in that movie, but he is almost always just playing Bill Murray. The way out is never easy.) They were either pure of heart, super dedicated, really smart, and/or willing to learn a lesson, so they got out of the time loop and survived the killer. Surviving something that was full of greed, wrath, fraud, violence, and all the rest would leave some emotional and possibly physical scars. The final girls most certainly have PTSD, and that is terrible, but they got out. They survived. They can try to rebuild, get some therapy, or maybe write a collection of essays about the experience in an effort to share with the world what it's like and show the world the way to survive. Maybe, with something like that, there can be more than just one final girl. Maybe, the horror movie just doesn't even have to happen. Maybe it can just be a normal dramedy about life. That would be so much better and healthier for everyone involved.

At the very end of *Inferno*, Virgil puts Dante on his back and carries him up on his ascent out of Hell. The journey wasn't the end for him. He didn't have to stay vengeful or commit more fraud or violence. He didn't have to be a traitor to those he left behind. He didn't have to leave anyone behind. He most certainly didn't have to stay in the center of Hell being eaten, head first, by Satan. Yes, I know what that sounds like. This isn't a smutty book even with all the fucks.

So please, climb on my back. We're almost done here.

If I had stayed at that job, I would be making almost 6 figures for 25 hours of work per week, working 30 weeks a year, but I walked away for a job that is not perfect by any stretch of the imagination. My university does dumb things and has stupid unwritten rules that make no sense without having any actual written rules for some things. It is a bureaucracy. There are still bullies, and there are still assholes. However, because there is no tenure, those people have no hold over me. I don't give a fuck what that asshole says because what he says doesn't control what I do. (OK, I do. I get mad a lot at dumb shit the assholes say. Hence the occasional day drink.)

I gave up the chance for a tenured job because the money wasn't worth it. I felt what I had to give up, which included but was not limited to my dignity and the respect of the important people in my life, was too much. I hated myself while I was working there. I gained over 20 pounds. I was constantly angry. I got caught up in office politics because they were everywhere, and there were no fucking doors to our offices. I heard every terrible thing everyone said about everyone else, including what they said about me. Fuck me. Doors were invented for a fucking reason.

So now, I teach double-digit courses year-round to make enough to live the life I want to live. I have much more responsibility at this job than I would if I stayed at the old job, but I am much healthier. I work out every day. I eat better. I sleep better. I think better. I am better. I am doing it because it is important. Higher education is a gateway to a better life for those who wish to try it. It most certainly was for me. The paradigm needs to flip. Students are the most important part of every university.

Everything we do, from the line cook in the cafeteria, to the 3rd shift campus safety worker, to the administrative assistant, to the President and the executive board, to the faculty both full- and part-time (instructors and Professors), should be about the students. They rely on us. They trust us. We need to respect that, and we need to quit the bullshit and the office politics and the name-calling behind it. Who cares what your title is? Who cares where you went to school? You're here now. These students in front of you need you, and you need them. Remember that.

Do better. Care more. It isn't about you. It is about them. If you don't want to be of service, hit the fucking road and go do something else. If you are a Professor, regardless of level or title, you are an expert in something. You are special, but you don't deserve special treatment. Your students and other faculty should respect you because you've earned it through your actions in the classroom and in the staff room, not because you have the most degrees or because you made it to the bottom ring of Hell.

I do my best to earn that respect every single day. Even though working in this field can feel like Hell, I am doing the job now for the same reason I did it when I walked into my first classroom all those years ago. I love it.

The Divine Comedy will continue with...

Academic Purgatory

BOOK CLUB QUESTIONS

1. Have you ever heard the term "adjunct Professor" before this book? What did you know?

2. Is this something you think colleges and universities should divulge to the students?

3. Do you think having an adjunct Professor changes the quality of the course? Why or Why not?

4. Do you think this practice is a good one? Why or why not?

5. What did you know about the professorial rankings? Provide your thoughts on the standard of professional rankings.

6. What do you think about tenure? Provide your thoughts on the practice of tenure.

7. What do you think of when you hear about higher education?

8. What do you think of the current state of higher education?

9. Do you think a college degree has the same value now as before? Explain.

10. Do you think that it matters what type of higher education one has? Does a technical degree or a liberal arts degree have more value right now?

AUTHOR BIO

VIRGIL HENRY

May you rest in pieces...
The Editor at 4HP

VIRGIL IS THE PRODUCT OF ADJUNCY SOCIETY and now lives in a tower of solitude with his twenty cats, collection of DVDs, and 90's posters.

More books from 4 Horsemen Publications

Literary & Short Story Collections

Cathleen Davies
Cheeky, Bloody Articles
And Marvel

Valerie Willis
Val's House of Musings: A Mixed
Genre Short Story Collection

Non-Fiction

Jörgen Jensen with Peter Lundgren
Mind Over Tennis: Mastering the
Mental Game

Lael Giebel
Sustainability is for Everyone:
Beginning Steps to Creating
a Sustainability Program for
Your Business

Josh Stehle
I Am A Suphero Expert: Growing Up
with my Autistic Brother

N.B. Johnson
Wonders and Miracles

Kiyomi Holland
HeARTwork

Coloring Books

Jenn Kotick
Mermaids

For Writers

4HP WRITER'S RESOURCES
The Author's Accountability Planner

MEGAN MACKIE
Advanced Con Quest

DR. JENIFER PAQUETTE
The General Worldbuilding Guide

VALERIE WILLIS
Writer's Bane: Research
Writer's Bane: Formatting 101

LETITIA WASHINGTON
The Psychology of Character Building
for Authors

Academia & Textbooks

**DR. JENIFER PAQUETTE &
LAURA MITA**
Sentence Diagramming 101: Fun with
Linguistics (and Movies)

TEXTBOOKS
Composition and Grammar: For
HCC by HCC

Discover more at

4HorsemenPublications.com

Printed in the USA
CPSIA information can be obtained
at www.ICGtesting.com
CBHW021536270924
14924CB00090B/466